A Straightforward Guide to Book-keeping and Accounts for Small Business

Tony Bannister

Straightforward Publishing Limited
38 Cromwell Road, London E17 9JN

First Edition 1995

British Library Cataloguing in Publication data. A catalogue record for this book is available from the British Library.

ISBN 1 89992 405 1

Printed by BPC Wheaton – Exeter
Cover design by Neil Grant, Front Line Graphics

A Straightforward Guide to Book-keeping and Accounts for Small Business

This book in the Straightforward Guides series is a practical introduction to the meaning and mechanics of book-keeping.

A Straightforward Guide to Book-keeping and Accounts for Small Business is written for people starting up a small business for the first time, whether as sole traders or in partnerships. No prior knowledge is presumed but emphasis is placed on why accurate books are important and how to keep them.

The book covers the following:-

* the importance of keeping financial books of record
* the single entry and the double entry systems of recording transactions
* which books to keep
* analysing the books
* petty cash recording
* VAT
* bank accounts and reconciliations
* book-keeping for partnerships
* the trial balance

The Author: Anthony Bannister was for many years a commercial accountant before becoming Accounts Manager for a City of London firm of Solicitors. He has written this book so that the business of running a small business will be easier for those with no prior financial skills.

Contents

INTRODUCTION TO THIS BOOK

You will not become an accountant by reading this book. Nor do you need to be one in order to make a success of running your own business. The aim of the book is to introduce the reader to the language and principles of book-keeping and accounts so that those who have already started their own small business or who are contemplating doing so in the future will gain the following benefits:–

i) confidence to begin and sustain the task of proper and accurate record-keeping;and

ii) sufficient knowledge of the basic principles that will enable them to do so in a manner that best suits their particular business;and

iii) an understanding of what their accountant is talking about when business accounts have to be drawn up; and iv)the determination to acquire a discipline essential for the control of their business.

The book is set out as follows:

Chapter one is an introduction to first principles. The distinction is emphasised between the individual as a private person from the proprietor of the business, where the business as a seperate public entity trades in Goods and/or Services and the private individual does not.

Chapter two deals with the books that should be kept, whatever the type of business, the recording of Cash or Credit sales and Purchases as the "Trading Accounts". Money as a flow in and out of the business; distinguishing the running expenses from other purchases. The Single Entry System and the Analysed Cashbook.

Chapter three introduces the Double Entry System for the more sophisticated business and the advantages of this method over the simpler Single Entry method, with illustrations.

Chapter four introduces the Trial Balance as the method to test the accuracy of your book-keeping; the component parts and what they are essential for. It also deals with the main types of error that can occur in compiling the trial balance.

Chapter five deals with using the books of account to prepare the Final Accounts – the Profit and Loss Account and the Balance Sheet.

Chapter six deals with accounting for Petty Cash and how this fits in with the overall system of control.

Chapter seven deals with accounting for Value Added Tax.

Chapter eight deals with checking the accuracy of the Internal Accounts with an External Control – the Bank Reconciliation.

Chapter nine deals with keeping the books of a small

Partnership, building on the same principles used by the Sole Trader.

At the end of this book you will find useful information about some of the professional and Statutory bodies that can offer further advice on the financial aspects of business.

Although this book cannot cover " everything you need to know" about the accounting side of your business, such as Taxation or the Law, it offers practical assistance to beginners to help them understand the basic principles and skills of book-keeping needed for efficient management.

If you have any comments concerning the contents and information in this book please do not hesitate to contact Straightforward Publishing at: 38 Cromwell Road, Walthamstow, London E17 9JN.

1

First Principles and Practice

The world is now a tougher place for businesses and unfortunately many fail. Apart from the fortunes of the market, the most common reasons are connected with what might be called sloppy management. Not paying attention to the routine but essential tasks can lead to the collapse of any business.

All businesses must therefore be managed, no matter what their size or complexity. Management means the control and co-ordination of all the constituent parts of a business – sales, purchases, production, distribution, credit, tax, etc. A common denominator is therefore necessary to explain and clarify the whole range of business activities, and that common denominator is money.

Spending money and receiving money is a constant process and each transaction must therefore be reduced to a monetary expression and then recorded in a Book of Account. The process of recording all this information relating to the financial affairs of the business is Book-Keeping.

The efficient management of the business will depend upon

effective financial management, the key to which is to set up and maintain a simple method of financial record-keeping best suited to the particular business, one which is intelligible to your accountant and acceptable to the statutory authorities who also have an interest in the financial affairs of proprietors and businesses – the Inland Revenue, the DSS and HM Customs & Excise.

Financial management means keeping track of all money coming in and going out, whether cash or cheque, where it comes from, where it goes to, how long it takes, what is being purchased and what is being sold.

For the individual planning to commence in business as a sole trader or enter into a small partnership there must be a Business Bank Account separate from the one in which personal money is handled.

Careful and regular scrutiny of the Business Bank Account Statements is a vital discipline – cross checking the books of account and the entries in them with those entries on the bank statements. You can make mistakes and so can your bank.

Every real transaction undertaken in the name of the business must be reflected by a financial transaction, evidenced by a financial piece of paper and entered in the books – somewhere.

Consider though a cash transaction that does not generate a formal financial document such as an invoice or till receipt, for example a parking meter payment.

In such a case you must create your own piece of paper to back up your claim that a business expense has been incurred. Transactions of this kind are best handled by the use of Petty Cash (dealt with in chapter 6). A petty cash Voucher, showing the date, amount spent and what it was spent on is necessary evidence to satisfy your Accountant that a business expense has been incurred, not a personal one, and that you are entitled to charge it to the business.

Being successful in a small business depends upon:–

i) The business making sufficient profit for the proprietor to withdraw that profit in order to meet his/her personal living costs as a minimum and satisfying his/her personal and financial ambitions as well. Profit means simply the residue of income after all expenses have been met.

ii) Knowing that the business is making a profit, by regular and methodical monitoring of the financial affairs of the business. If you don't know this then in the commercial climate of today you are living in a dream world and the business will fail.

iii) Showing how you know this by keeping accurate books of account. Ideally you should do this on an ongoing basis, at the very least once a week. This may seem a lot to expect, when most of your time and energy is and should be going into getting the business off the ground, but it is not. Acquiring an essential management habit may take a little time. A bad habit can take even longer to lose, by which time it may be too late.

If you are so busy that a mountain of paper accumulates in a shoebox over several months then you must employ a book-keeper to update the books. This is especially so if all or part of your business is a cash business.

Keeping the books regularly and up to date is not difficult. Not keeping them well or at all means you are not taking care of the business. Trying to sort out a mess later will cost more money when the time comes for your Accountant to prepare the final accounts.

The key concept is Control.

An important part of control is taking yourself seriously. Well kept books of account reflect and underpin a well-run business. Badly kept books indicate a lack of control on the part of the business person, a lack of control that may well spill over into other aspects of the business.

YOU AND YOUR BUSINESS

This section could be entitled "It's only money, and it's mine".

To which the answer is "Not necessarily".

It must be clearly understood that your business is some "thing" that you have created, separate from yourself and must be treated as such.

If you are a sole trader (or sole proprietor), this may sound strange at first, but think of it this way.

Every year you will have to get your business accounts drawn up by an accountant, unless your income falls below a certain low threshold. In any event you will have to submit accounts of some description to the Inland Revenue.

During that year you will have drawn out money from the business for your personal use. You will have recorded this in the books as e.g. "Drawings", or "Personal Drawings". Let us suppose that over the year drawings amount to £10,000. Nobody is concerned what you have spent the money on – clothes, food, holidays, entertainment etc. Why? Because such expenditure is nothing to do with business activities.

For the same reason you must separate your personal expenditure from the funds flowing in and out of your business. Suppose as an individual you spend £500 on a holiday. If this money is to be paid to you by the business, it will have been recorded as a drawing on the business . What you spend the money on is of no concern to the business because taking a holiday is not a business activity. Suppose you decide to save the £500, instead of spending it. Again saving your personal money is not a business activity. You may decide at some later date to put the £500 back into the business by way of a

"Capital" injection. The sum then represents part of your personal stake in the business as one of your personal assets or investments, in much the same way as having bought premium bonds, or shares in a Limited Company.

These points are even more important if you are a member of a partnership, along with one or more others, even if they are family members. The business as a partnership is a separate entity from you as an individual and separate from your partners. Partnerships are dealt with in chapter 9 and may operate with reference to a formal written Agreement, in the absence of which they are governed by Law, principally the Partnership Act of 1890.

Likewise if you decide at a later stage to run your business as a Limited Company, you are required by law to separate your personal financial affairs from those of the Company.

Book-keeping and Accounts for Limited Companies are not dealt with in this book, but the same common sense commercial principles are equally appropriate.

Whether or not to record your personal expenditure and savings in detailed books of account is entirely your personal concern. The financial transactions of your business must be recorded in properly maintained books of account, to which we now turn.

2

THE BOOKS TO KEEP

Your business activities will consist of selling goods and/or services.

At the same time you will have to spend money on behalf of the business, on the purchase or rent of premises, raw materials, equipment, stationery etc. in order to conduct business.

Remember that every business transaction generates a financial transaction, all of which must be recorded in books of account on an ongoing basis. It is a fundamental management requirement that this be done on a regular basis, at a minimum once a week. Leave it much longer, and sooner or later an iron law of accounting will come into operation. You will have mislaid a financial record or simply forgotten to request one or issue one. When you do get around to updating the books, they won't balance. Unless you can discover the error before the end of the financial year your accountant will be faced with the task of reconciling "incomplete records", which he or she will enjoy because of the professional challenge but which costs you more money for more of his/her time.

WHAT INFORMATION MUST BE KEPT?

As a minimum you must keep records of the following:–

i) All the invoices raised (or rendered) on behalf of the business, either when the goods are delivered or the services supplied, or shortly afterwards. An invoice is a legal document and constitutes a formal demand for money. It must provide enough information to identify the business which sent it, who it was sent to, what it is for and whether VAT is payable.

ii) A list of your Sales invoices, numbered sequentially.

iii)All Purchase invoices received, and listed i.e. those demands made on your business for the payment of money.

iv)Wages and salaries paid, and to whom; Income tax and NI contributions paid over to the Tax authorities.

v) All cheque-book stubs, paying-in slips/books, counterfoils of petty cash vouchers, business bank account statements. Without these you cannot compile your books of account.

vi)A full record of VAT, whether paid by or paid to the business.

THE ADVANTAGES OF A BOOK-KEEPING SYSTEM FOR YOUR BUSINESS

a) To provide accurate information sufficient to assess whether you are managing the business at a profit or a loss, or whether the business is solvent i.e. is there enough cash available in the business to pay all the outstanding liabilities on demand? The right information of the right kind at the right time is a vital management tool. Good management means making informed decisions of the right kind at the right time based on information that is true and therefore trustworthy.

b) To provide the information required for correct assessments of VAT and Income Tax, so as to avoid financial penalties (and possibly a suspect reputation) for incorrect and/or late payments. HM Customs & Excise keep records for seven years and the Inland Revenue keep them for three years, and so must you. Your accountant will need the best information in order to minimise your tax liabilities, unless of course you decide to submit a statement of income to your Inspector of Taxes without recourse to an accountant. In any event the Inspector will require a calculation of your Income from the business in the form of an Income and Expenditure Account for each trading year.

c) To monitor the behaviour of the business over time by reference to financial summaries "at a glance". You don't need to remember for example how many meals were served in your restaurant business say in the month of July 1995 compared with July 1994. The comparison that matters is the financial one with reference to the value of those transactions.

HOW TO RECORD THE INFORMATION YOU NEED

There are basically four methods of book-keeping. Which one to choose will depend largely on the type and size of business you have established. Take advice from a business adviser or accountant if you are unsure as to which is the best one for your needs.

a) Proprietary systems.

These are best suited for sole traders in cash transaction types of business e.g. jobbing builders, market traders or some small shopkeepers. This type of business requires daily record keeping, often including till-rolls for the cash till and offers a simple method of control over finances.

A number of pre-printed stationery systems are available at

business bookshops. Select one that allows you enough space to record all that needs recording. Worked examples are set out at the beginning of each book to show you how to keep cash records and the bank position, which can be calculated by following the instructions included.

A list of business stationery systems publishers is found at the end of the book.

Cash businesses are more vulnerable than other types for the following reasons:–

i) It is far easier to lose or misplace paperwork. Therefore it is easier to lose control and lose money. Therefore it is more difficult to plan for the future.

ii) It is far more difficult to separate the cash that belongs in the business from the cash belonging to the proprietor.

iii)The Inland Revenue and HM Customs & Excise pay far closer attention to cash businesses because of the greater scope for "creative accounting" and tax evasion.

To minimise these risks, cash business-proprietors are strongly advised to pay their daily cash takings into the bank by using pre-printed paying-in books supplied by their bank. It is also vital to obtain receipts for purchases made from the takings and to keep them in an orderly fashion.

b) The Analysed Cash Book System.

This is perhaps the most common method used by small businesses selling mostly on credit, with perhaps some cash sales. It relies on the Single Entry system of book-keeping, where each entry is, as the name implies, made once only, and all entries are made in one book, the Cashbook. The analysed cashbook is the "bible" of the business. It allows "at a glance" analysis because it is arranged on a columnar basis, showing how much has been received into the business, when and from where, how much of each receipt is attributable to VAT and therefore how much is the net amount belonging to the business. All this information is written up on one side of a pre-printed book, the left-hand page, showing all monies paid into the bank on behalf of the business. On the opposite, right-hand page are set out in separate columns details of what has been spent by the business, in other words, monies paid out of the bank, to whom and when.

This system is explained and illustrated in greater detail later in this chapter.

c) The Double Entry System

This method of recording accounts relies on ledgers, or separate books of account for each type of transaction. Far greater detail and control are possible using this system. As well as a cash account there is scope for setting up other ledgers such as the bought ledger for purchases, sales ledger, nominal (or business expense) ledger, salaries and so on.

It is much easier to monitor how much has been spent over a period of time on each type of transaction, simply by referring to the particular ledger or account, on each of which a running balance is struck. Every transaction is recorded in the major account called the Cash Account and also in them appropriate subsidiary ledger. In this way the Cash Account acts as a "Control" account for all the separate accounts of the business. The most important feature of this system is the characterisation of all book-keeping entries as either a "credit" ("he trusts" i.e." the business owes him") or "debit" ("he owes"). The sophistication of this method lies in the use of two entries for each transaction.

For each credit entry in the Cash Account there must be a

corresponding debit entry for the same amount in a different account. Likewise for each debit entry in the Cash Account there must be a corresponding credit entry in a different account. The key words are "equal and opposite". That way the greatest possible degree of control is obtained.

This system is explained and illustrated in greater detail in chapter 3.

d) Computerised Accounting Systems

A wide variety of off-the-shelf packages are available, which rely on single or double entry methods. It may be tempting to invest in an accounts package at the outset, especially if you intend to use other computer packages in the business. It would be most unwise to start using such a package without understanding the principles that underlie them. Businesses have failed because of the familiar – "GIGO" – garbage in, garbage out. Money is the lifeblood of the business so don't turn it into garbage by neglecting an understanding of the what, why and how of book-keeping.

THE SINGLE ENTRY SYSTEM OF BOOK-KEEPING AND THE ANALYSED CASHBOOK

You will need to record the following financial information – for the efficient management of the business and for your accountant, in order to prepare the accounts of the business at the year's end:–

i) monies coming into the business from all sources – Income from Sales and other kinds of Receipts not derived from Sales i.e. INCOME and RECEIPTS; and

ii) monies going out of the business to all destinations i.e. PAYMENTS and EXPENSES.

From these aggregate accounts can be ascertained the following:–

* Value of sales per month
* Value of receipts from other sources
* Value of VAT

Looking at Income & Receipts first, consider the following information extracted from the Cashbook of "Diana's Fashions", a sole proprietorship. Diana buys fabrics, makes dresses and sells them to dress shops and in street markets.

During the course of the month she recorded the following:–

Payments and Expenses

Date	Cheque no.	Details	£
Nov			
02	00046	Lyn's Haberdashery	96.00
03	00047	Sid's Fabrics	123.00
03	00048	British Telecom	95.99
12	00049	Lloyd's Bank: cash	100.00
12	00050	London Press	17.50
12	00051	Lloyd's: Petty cash	83.50
22	00052	Smart's Manufactures	10.75
25	00053	Green Agency: rent	300.00
28	00054	W H Smith	15.25
30	00055	Smart's Manufactures	115.00
30	00056	Joan Wilson: wages	85.00

Also in the same month she recorded the following

Income and Receipts

Date	Receipt no.	Details	£
Nov			
04	23	Building Soc. Transfer	400.00
09	24	Market Takings (9 Nov)	204.00
09	25	S. Jones: Invoice 92	575.00
16	26	Market Takings (15 Nov)	165.00
16	27	J. Slade: Invoice 83	328.00
23	28	Market Takings (23 Nov)	301.00
30	29	Market Takings (29 Nov)	342.00
30	30	M. Howes: Invoice 71	750.00
30	31	Market Takings (30 Nov)	210.00
30	32	A. Smith: Invoice 98	115.00

These entries are set out in her Cashbook for the month thus, showing how they are analysed, column by column:–

INCOME AND RECEIPTS

These entries always appear on the left hand side of each page of the cashbook.

First note the entry "Transfer from Building Society – £400.00.

This shows a transfer from Diana's Personal account into the business – a transfer of Capital. It has been included to illustrate the fact that the business account is separate from her personal account. The business now "owes" Diana £400 (hopefully temporarily), presumably because of a perceived risk of overdrawing the business account. This situation could arise because:

Date	Details	Folio	Total	Net Cash Sales	Net Invoice Sales	Transfers	VAT
Nov 04	Building Society Trf	23	400.00			400.00	
Nov 09	Market Takings 9/11	24	204.00	173.62			30.38
Nov 09	S. Jones: Invoice 92	25	575.00		489.36		85.64
Nov 16	Market Takings 15/11	26	165.00	140.42			24.58
Nov 16	J. Slade Invoice 83	27	328.00		279.15		48.85
Nov 23	Market Takings 23/11	28	301.00	256.17			44.83
Nov 30	Market Takings 29/11	29	342.00	291.06			50.94
Nov 30	M. Howes: Invoice 71	30	210.0	178.72			31.28
Nov 30	A. Smith: Invoice 98	32	115.00		97.87		17.13
			3390.00	1039.99	1504.68	400.00	445.33

i) entering up her books on a daily basis she therefore knew in advance that the business would dip into overdraft. She could not anticipate her market takings on later dates in the month and at the same time knew that she had to meet expenses on behalf of the business, as indicated in the illustration.

ii alternatively she had received word from the bank forewarning her of an overdraft situation in her business account.

What has not been shown in the illustration is the "Balance brought forward" from the previous month. Had this been in substantial credit she may not have had to make the transfer from her own funds. It has been assumed that this was not the case in order to emphasise the importance of prudence in the management of what is substantially a cash business, dependent upon market trading for most of the income.

All entries in the cashbook need to be adequately identified.

A transfer needs to be identified as a Loan in a "Transfer" column, if indeed it is such, in which case it will have to be repaid at a later stage. On the other hand it may be intended to be long-term, i.e. for more than a year, in which case it probably then represents a contribution of Capital to the business. The business again "owes" Diana £400, because we are dealing with two separate financial entities.

Notice the distinction made in two separate columns between "Cash sales" receipts and "Invoice sales" receipts for earlier sales made by granting credit to customers. This is made again because Diana Fashions is a part credit/part cash business. By showing the two separately she is able to monitor the progress of the two kinds of trading. Apart from a natural "feel" she would undoubtedly develop for this aspect of her business she is able to prove it by reference to her cashbook.

By identifying the number of each invoice against payment she can cross-reference these payments to an Invoice Book, which simply lists all invoices raised, in consecutive number sequence. Upon payment of an invoice she can mark it off against her list, showing at a glance which remain outstanding, and which if any have been part-paid only.

The only other kind of Income or Receipt into the business, apart from Sales, loans or capital contributions, would derive from the sale of unwanted physical assets such as second hand equipment.

CREDIT CONTROL

This is the term used for monitoring payments and comparing them against invoices still outstanding, which invoices reflect the amount of credit the business has granted to its debtors. The emphasis is on the word "Control". Without regular attention to this aspect of the business control will be more difficult to maintain and can eventually be lost.

So long as the book-keeping is updated regularly Diana will know

i) what invoices have been raised and who for;

ii) which have been paid, fully or in part;

iii) which remain outstanding;

iv) how long they have been outstanding;

v) how much she is owed by debtors of the business.

So long as she has this information and trusts it to be accurate she is in a position to make an informed decision about what she then needs to do about each outstanding invoice. She will also know just how much of the working capital of the business has been extended to debtors.

Returning to the cashbook, it can be seen at a glance how much has been received and what the individual amounts and the totals for the month represent. This is achieved simply by extending the arithmetical entry across the page and writing in the sum in the appropriate column.

EXPENSES/PAYMENTS *see page opposite.*

This side of the cashbook uses the same method of showing the total amounts paid, a referencing system based upon cheque numbers and extensions of the sums across the page into separate columns. The right hand side of the page is always used because there will always be a greater number of different destinations of payments than there will be for receipts, and all books are printed with more columns on the right hand side than on the left. All pre-printed books, and loose-leaf sheets, will follow this layout.

To avoid possible later confusion, and to maximise the information available to your accountant, enter as much information as possible in the "Details" or narrative column. Also remember to enter the date a cheque is drawn and the cheque number, in the respective columns, as shown.

The number of columns used will obviously depend upon the complexity of the business and therefore the number of types of transaction that occur.

Always use a cashbook that contains more columns than you need for day-to-day transactions. Publishers of business accounts stationery produce a wide range of alternatives, from 2 column books to 42 column books. These are coded to indicate the number of columns, e.g. 5/14, 5/16 and 5/18 being among the most common ones sold. The first figure indicates the number of columns on the Receipts side of the page and the second figure, the number of columns on the Expenses/Payments side.

Expenses / Payments

Date	Details	Cheque No.	Total	Stock	Telephone	Publicity	Drawings	Petty Cash	Rent	Stationery	Wages	VAT
Nov 02	Lyn's Haberdashery	00046	96.00	81.70								14.30
Nov 02	Sid's Fabrics	00047	123.00	104.68								18.32
Nov 03	British Telecom	00048	95.99		81.69							14.30
Nov 12	Lloyds Bank: Cash	00049	100.00				100.00					
Nov 12	London Press	00050	17.50			14.90						2.60
Nov 12	Lloyds: Petty Cash	00051	83.50					83.50				
Nov 22	Smarts Manufacture	00052	10.75	9.15								1.60
Nov 25	Green Agency: rent	00053	300.00						300.00			
Nov 28	WH Smith	00054	15.25							12.98		2.27
Nov 30	Smarts Manufacture	00055	115.00	97.87								17.13
Nov 30	John Wilton: Wages	00056	85.00								85.00	
			1041.99	293.40	81.69	14.90	100.00	83.50	300.00	12.98	85.00	70.52

In the course of a trading year the majority of trading expenses will be those that have been anticipated, such as rent for premises. You may have attempted an estimate for other known heads of expenditure, such as telephones and postage, or the running costs of a delivery van.

Although it can be difficult to estimate accurately how much will be spent on each head, you should be able to identify the types of expenditure you know will be incurred. If you are unsure about this then your accountant can advise. Do not sail into a business venture without first doing your homework!

Note particularly the following division of expenses into Non-trading and Trading expenses:–

A) NON-TRADING EXPENSES

Capital Equipment

In the cashbook you need to record expenditure on any non-trading expense, i.e. capital items such as machinery or computer equipment. The purchase price of such items must be recorded separately from any running costs, even though all financial outlays of whatever kind are recorded in the cashbook as expenses.

Non-trading expenditure does not form part of the Profit & Loss account, and is recorded by convention in the final column of the cashbook. This column can be identified as e.g. "Capital", or "Sundries", and an adequate note made alongside the entry to explain what each entry represents.

B) TRADING EXPENSES

All heads of expenditure connected with running the business are Trading Expenses, including VAT.

Aggregated, they form one section of the equation needed to calculate the profit or loss at the end of the financial year. They are examined more fully in chapter 5, which deals with the Final Accounts, one of which is the Profit & Loss Account. The other part of the Final Accounts is called the Balance Sheet.

As well as regular anticipated types of expense there will sometimes be irregular expenditure on anticipated items of a non-capital nature, possibly occurring only once in a trading year. These would include Insurance premiums, if paid annually. Accordingly there might be a column kept open for "Insurances". A similar case arises with Business Rates, which are payable either in one annual amount or in 10 equal instalments.

More regular heads of expense might include some of the following, for each of which a separate column will be needed:

Salaries and Wages

It is advisable to pay salaries or wages by cheque. Wages can be recorded separately in a Wages Account book so long as they are also entered in the cashbook, especially if they are paid on a regular basis. Always identify in the Details column the name of the person(s) you pay, for ease of reference to your Wages Book.

Naturally you will have to pay Income Tax and National Insurance contributions, as deducted from gross salaries/wages. Such payments will be recorded in separate columns, which are not shown in the example.

Rent

Payments of Rent should also include the time period to which it refers, e.g. the month or the quarter year.

VAT

The "Total" column for each payment shows the gross figure as is recorded on the cheque stub, and includes any VAT. If you are registered for VAT then this can be reclaimed. VAT must be separately accounted for. Accordingly there must be a column to show the VAT element of the expenditure. VAT is dealt with in chapter 7. Briefly, if your aggregated Turnover i.e. sales income, reaches or is expected to reach a prescribed threshold level during the course of the year then you must register for VAT. Because the rate is at a high level (currently 17.5%) it is a significant proportion of the cash flowing in and out of a business.

Petty Cash

You will almost certainly need to spend small sums of cash, often on a daily basis, on behalf of the business. These payments are quite separate from your own personal cash expenditure on such trivia as clothes, entertainment or food for the weekend.

Petty cash for the business is drawn from the bank by cheque in the same way as any other item of expense, as shown in our example. Petty Cash is dealt with more fully in chapter 6.

Drawings

Apart from monies flowing in and out of the business as a consequence of trading and recorded in the cashbook , it should not be forgotten that the whole purpose of the exercise is to provide you, the owner, with a living .

Since the business is likely to be your sole source of personal income, you will need to withdraw income from it during the course of trading for the purposes of meeting your personal commitments. You cannot live on nothing until the end of the financial year in anticipation of enough profit from the business for the preceding 12 months. Drawings will be offset against the profits of the business, as calculated at the end of the business financial year and declared to the Inland Revenue.

The "Drawings" column shows the amounts of money drawn out from the business i.e. paid to the proprietor by the business. Therefore it constitutes a business "expense" just as clearly as any other item of business expense, such as wages or salaries paid to employees. It is not however to be confused with these because the owner of the business (i.e. you) is not an "employee" of the business if it is a sole tradership or a partnership. You might become an employee of your own business only if it is set up as a Limited Company.

In summary, every expense incurred by the business is entered into the Expenses/Payments side of the cashbook. These include payments for purchases of materials and/or stock, bought for resale by the business.

Payments are arranged in columns to group together types of purchase, for the purposes of control and analysis.

At the end of a period of trading, monthly, quarterly, half-yearly and annually, it is then a straightforward exercise to calculate ongoing costs, type by type. Following the reconciliation of the cashbook to the bank at the end of each month, thereby proving the accuracy of the book-keeping entries, the "bottom line " figures are then transferred forward to become the opening balances for the subsequent month. Bank reconciliations are dealt with in chapter 8.

3

The Accounts to Keep

Technically speaking, "Book-keeping" means the recording of business transactions in Books of Account.

"Accounting" means taking financial information from the books of account and using it to explain and understand the financial position of the business.

This chapter explores more fully the relationship between the two functions, by introducing the Double Entry system of book-keeping and the creation of accounts maintained separately from the cash account.

THE DOUBLE ENTRY SYSTEM

This method is fundamentally different to the Single Entry/ Analysed Cashbook system in which, as we have seen, all financial transactions are recorded in one book of account.

Nevertheless, the Double Entry method follows the same procedures of money management as in the single entry/cashbook method. Payments into the bank of cash and cheque are made the same day of receipt, and all payments out of the business are made by cheque, or by cash from petty cash.

Using this method, one account, called the "Cash Account", is used to record all banking entries i.e. all monies received into and all cheque payments for monies going out of the business. The Cash Account therefore acts as what can be called a "Control Account". All other entries can be related back to the Cash Account for checking and control purposes. As noted in chapter 2 this is because for every entry made in the Cash Account a second equal and opposite entry for the same amount must be made in a separate account.

The Double Entry system also relies upon each entry being either a Credit or Debit entry. Credit means "he owes" (to the business), and Debit means "he trusts", (i.e. the business owes him). So the second leg of the system works as noted also in chapter 2. For every credit entry in the Cash Account the corresponding entry in the other account must be a debit. Likewise, for every debit entry in the Cash Account the corresponding entry in the other account must be a credit.

This explains how the Internal control mechanism works within the business.

All Cash Account entries are reflected in banking entries which are shown eventually on the bank statements of the business. The bank therefore acts as the External "Control" account for the business, as seen from the Cash Account.

Since the bank also employs the Double entry system of recording its accounts with its customers, the double entry system operates between the bank and the Cash account of your business.

It therefore follows that for every credit entry in your cash account the corresponding entry in the Bank's account of the business must be a debit entry. Likewise for every debit entry in your cash account the corresponding entry in the Bank's account of the business must be a credit entry.

Every time you receive a cheque or cash in payment for the supply of goods and/or services, you pay it into the bank on behalf of the business. On the Bank statement that is eventually received, such payments are recorded by the bank as "Credits".

Therefore, and according to the double entry system of book-keeping, the corresponding entries for payments received must be recorded in the Cash account as "Debits". Paradoxical but logical.

Looking at the relationship between any entry shown on the bank statement and the same entry shown in an internal account, it follows that these will be identical, as to whether they are Credits or Debits, since the account "in between" (the Cash Account) will be the opposite.

To take a simple example from the illustration of a business in the previous chapter – Diana's Fashions.

She sells some dresses to an existing customer on credit and then receives payment by cheque.

She pays the cheque into the bank and the entry shows up on the bank statement the following week as a Credit, since she now has more money in the bank than previously.

The corresponding entry on her Cash account must therefore be a Debit entry for cash received, according to the double entry method.

A Debit entry on her Cash account therefore requires a corresponding Credit entry on another internal account, in this case the account of the customer and identified as such e.g. Susan's Dress Shop A/c.

Again if she buys stationery on credit, her stock of stationery increases, as does its monetary value, and the amount that she owes to the supplier increases by a corresponding amount. One entry is shown as a credit and the other as a debit.

It is unwise to attempt to set up a double entry system of book-keeping without having understood the fundamental theoretical and practical essentials. Many people possess all the necessary entrepreneurial and product knowledge skills for success in business. At the same time many retain a mild (or severe) phobia of book-keeping, accounts and all things to do with numbers. Hopefully by now any phobias have been alleviated, if not dispelled.

Whichever system you use, your books will form the basis of the Final Accounts of the business, which are dealt with in chapter 5.

TYPES OF ACCOUNT

Accounting convention requires that all internal accounts be classified according to the following description:–

1) Personal Accounts

These record transactions with particular customers, i.e. those with whom the business regularly deals. A separate customer account is kept in the name of each customer.

2) Nominal Accounts

These record the Expenses incurred in running the business and the Income generated from sales .Again a separate account is maintained for each type of expense, e.g. electricity, business rates, stationery, telephones, postage etc. Likewise separate accounts are also kept for income from different sources.

3) Real Accounts

These accounts are kept for assets and their different types, e.g. office furniture, computer equipment, vehicles etc.

Such Accounts are sometimes referred to as "Ledgers", as an alternative mode of description.

With every type of account – Personal, Nominal or Real, each financial transaction is recorded in the separate sub-account to which it relates as well as in the main Cash account.

Accounts can be illustrated as follows:

Name of Account

1. Date	Details/Narrative	Debit	Credit	Balance

2. FURNITURE AND FITTINGS ACCOUNT

Date	Details/narrative	Debit	Credit	Balance
Nov 1	Cash A/C	400.00		(400.00)

3. TELEPHONE ACCOUNT

Date	Details/Narrative	DR	CR	Balance
Nov 3	Cash A/C	142.00	(142.00)	

4. CASH ACCOUNT

Date	Details/Narrative	DR	CR	Balance
Balance b/fwd				(3400.00)
Nov 1	Furn/Fittings A/C		400.00	3000.00
Nov 3	Telephones A/C		142.00	2858.00

And so on and so on, creating a separate account for each type of expense, and making corresponding entries on the Cash account for each entry made on a named account.

A useful way to treat book-keeping is to view it as a special language, with its own unique vocabulary and rules of grammar. One common rule is that the term Credit is often abbreviated to CR, and Debit abbreviated to DR, as shown above.

Furthermore, It is a fundamental rule that all accounts show Debit entries on the left hand side and Credit entries on the right hand side. All bank statements adhere to the same convention. A simple way to remember this is that there is an "R" in Credit and an "R" in Right, so "Credits go on the Right, right?".

All accounts fit into one of four different categories, as follows

1) INCOME. We have already seen examples.

2) EXPENSES. We have already seen examples.

3) ASSETS

Examples include: Furniture; Vehicles; Buildings; Leases; Computers; Stock; Cash in hand; Cash at bank; Work in Progress (part finished products); Debtors (Customers who have not yet paid for goods/services supplied/delivered).

Assets are in fact what is "Owned" by the business, at any particular time.

4) LIABILITIES

These describe what the business "Owes" to others, and include:

- Trade Creditors: those suppliers owed money by the business for goods/services already supplied/delivered but not yet paid for.

- Accrued Expenses: expenses relating to the current period for which no invoice has yet been received from the supplier and for which payment is not yet due, but which you know will become payable in the future, e.g. a telephone account which straddles two accounting periods.
- Bank Overdraft: The bank's money, which does not belong to the business and will have to be repaid, either on demand or on a negotiated date.

Assets and liabilities will be collated and appear as the Balance Sheet of the business, and will include one other figure from the second main account, the Profit and Loss Account.

This will be either the profit or loss of the business for the period, calculated by subtracting the aggregate Expenses from the aggregate Income for the same period.

This is because a profit represents an additional amount of capital available to the business and a loss represents a reduction in the amount of capital available. In any event, all capital items and changes to the capital used in the business are displayed in the Balance Sheet.

This equation can be illustrated as follows:–

a) INCOME
minus EXPENSES
= PROFIT or LOSS

---

b) ASSETS +PROFIT/–LOSS
minus LIABILITIES
= NET ASSETS

These equations represent the basic formulae for calculating the overall financial position of the business, utilising every single account, or ledger, referred to earlier in the four categories. These formulae will be elaborated upon in the course of chapter 5 (the Final Accounts).

To compile the Profit and Loss Account and the Balance Sheet requires a simple exercise of collating all the closing balances on all the accounts at the end of the Accounting Period (the financial year of the business) and arranging them into their appropriate categories.

Below are a few examples of important adjustments to accounts that may need to be made in order to provide accuracy.

DEBTORS

This is the term used to describe those who owe money to the business. Debtors represent an asset of a business and therefore appear only in the Balance Sheet.

You will have adopted one of two methods to record and monitor the situation with debtors.

a) You may have "lumped" them all together in one aggregateDebtors Account; or

b) Separated them out into named Debtor accounts, so as to more closely monitor the comparative progress of each and to maintain closer control of the most important. At the end of the year, in order to compile a summary of debtors, you will need to collate the final balances on each separate account to arrive at an aggregate Debtors account.

BAD AND DOUBTFUL DEBTS

At the end of the year there will almost certainly be customers who have not paid what they owe when the Final Accounts are compiled. Some of those debts will be paid during the course of the following financial year.

But you may have doubts as to whether they will all be paid in full, or when.

Are there some debts which are very old and about which you are unsure about eventual payment?

Have you spent time and effort in fruitless attempts at recovery?

Have you gone so far as to instruct Solicitors to commence legal proceedings for recovery?

Have any of the debtors of the business become insolvent/ "disappeared"?

If the answer to any of these questions is yes, or possibly, or probably, then either a Bad or a Doubtful debt has arisen. You will have to take a view as to which outstanding debts fall into each category because you will need to make separate provisions for each in the final accounts.

Many business people are reluctant to take firm action for recovery of either a sum outstanding or for the return of goods supplied. Many others will take whatever action they deem necessary to effect recovery of one or the other. In any event it is not possible to effect the return of a service rendered, for the obvious reason that nothing tangible can be physically recovered.

Whether to try for recovery or not is a practical decision, governed by the circumstances of the time and the inclination of the proprietor.

In the accounts, successful recovery of a debt means that the Debtors account must be reduced, because the cash in hand or cash at the bank will have been increased. Successful recovery of the goods means once again that the Debtors account must be reduced, because the Stock account will have been increased. The double entry system at work - any credit to one account must be matched by a corresponding debit to another account.

If neither the debt nor the goods can be recovered then the remaining option is to cut your losses and write-off the debt from the books. In this case the sum becomes a Bad Debt and must be treated in the appropriate way.

First the bad debt must be transferred from the Debtors account, since it is no longer an asset, to a Bad Debt account.

Since Bad debts will be shown as DR or Debit entries, it follows that the entries to reduce the Debtors account will be CR or Credit entries, in accordance with the double entry rules.

Bad debts are those you are sure will not be paid, nor any goods recovered, in all probability because the debtor has gone out of business or, formally or informally, you have been told you wont be paid.

Bad Debts by definition do not appear on the Balance Sheet because they have been removed from the Debtors account.

The write-off does appear in the Profit and Loss account as a Bad Debt Expense because it is an Expense or cost that the business has incurred in the current period.

Doubtful Debts are different. They are by implication those you are not sure about.

Again the procedure is to create a special account by transferring doubtful debts to a "Doubtful Debt Provision Account". The balance on this account will be shown separately as set-off (or subtracted from) the Debtors account in the Balance Sheet, which will then indicate the net amount believed to be collectable.

Any provision for doubtful debts will also appear as an item in the Profit and Loss account as a "Doubtful Debt Provision", as an Expense, because it represents an anticipated though not yet proven Expense that will be borne by the business.

Again, like the Bad Debt account, a Doubtful Debt Provision account will show DR or Debit entries, according to the double entry rules.

DISHONOURED CHEQUES

It is possible that these will occur from time to time and may eventually turn out to be either bad or doubtful debts.

Until the situation is clearer, upon re-presentation and clearance through the banking system, these are best taken out of the books altogether. This is effected simply by reversing the entries already made to the cash account and in the other corresponding account.

DEPRECIATION OF ASSETS

This is a technical subject best left to your accountant to calculate.

Briefly it refers to the process of writing-off a proportion of the value of physical assets every year of their useful life, to reflect the fact that the assets will be "used up" over a period of years. The Book Values will eventually diminish to zero, even if assets are still in use. It is beyond the scope of this book to explain the different methods and tax implications of Depreciation.

Suffice it to say that it is shown in the Profit and Loss account as an expense, or annual "cost" to the business, and also in the Balance Sheet as a set-off or subtraction from the original value of each asset.

In the Balance Sheet however both annual depreciation and depreciation "Accumulated" over each asset's lifetime is shown, to calculate the current, book value, or net worth of each asset.

Further refinements relate to the treatment of Capital introduced into the business by the proprietor and to Drawings out of the business by the proprietor. These issues will be dealt with more fully in chapter 5. At this stage, to complete the introduction, it is sufficient to remind ourselves that Capital is always treated as an Asset, and therefore appears as a Balance Sheet item, while Drawings are a specific form of Expense to the business and therefore appear in the Profit and Loss account.

Let us return to the Bank Statement referred to earlier showing how it operates as the External "Control" account for the business.

See table opposite.

Assuming that the business bank account is in Credit, not a debit or overdraft situation, then this credit position must appear as a debit balance in the Cashbook, since the Cashbook is a mirror image of the bank's treatment of the account. To further illustrate the theory, if the account of the business at the bank is in credit, the cash balance to the credit of the business represents a Liability of the bank to the business.

The bank's liability to the business represents an asset of the business, so assets are shown in the cashbook as DRs, which we have already seen with reference to payments-in of cheques and/ or cash.

The bank statement shows a number of transactions, each of which serves to increase or decrease the balance held, and we are all familiar with the format used. Our illustration shows that a credit balance is maintained throughout.

The first entry shows a credit balance brought forward from the previous page.

The second entry shows a payment of "Cheque & cash" into the account, shown obviously as a credit. Therefore this entry will appear in the cashbook of Diana's Fashions as a Debit or DR.

In this way the bank statement acts as the External Control account of the business.

X Bank

Statement of Account

Account 2136 6987	Diana Smith T/a Diana's Fashions Address	Page 2 Date 30-Nov-95
Sort code 51 00 03		

Date	Reference	Dr	Cr	Bal	
01-Nov-95	B/f			49.00	CR
01-Nov-95	chq & cash		290.00	339.00	CR
05-Nov-95	00046	96.00		243.00	CR
05-Nov-95	00048	95.99		147.01	CR
12-Nov-95	00047	123.00		24.01	CR
12-Nov-95	chq & cash				CR
16-Nov-95	chq & cash				CR
17-Nov-95	000				CR
18-Nov-95	000				CR
18-Nov-95	000				CR
18-Nov-95	000				CR
19-Nov-95	000				CR
19-Nov-95	chq & cash				CR
28-Nov-95	chq & cash				CR
28-Nov-95	000				CR
28-Nov-95	000				CR
28-Nov-95	000				CR
30-Nov-95	000				CR
30-Nov-95	chq & cash				CR
30-Nov-95	Interest		12.00		CR
30-Nov-95	Bank charges	4.00			CR

Total debits	Total credits

Since the Cash Account acts as the Internal Control account of the business, for every entry on the Cash Account it follows that there must be a corresponding opposing entry on an account within the business. The £290 is shown on the cash account as a DR so a corresponding CR entry must appear on an internal account as well, in this case the Debtor's account. Again, because of the double entry system, when an invoice was originally raised for the sale a DR entry was effected on the account of the debtor and a CR entry effected on the Sales account.

The third entry shows a DR against the cheque number, indicating that a cheque paid out on behalf of the business has been duly presented and cleared. In the cashbook therefore we would expect to see a CR entry of £96.00. If the bank statement related to the transactions shown in our example in chapter 2 we know that the payment was for material bought from Lyn's Haberdashery (in chapter 2) therefore the entry would appear as a DR to Lyn's Haberdashery account, representing a reduction previously owed i.e. a reduction in a trade creditor liability to Lyn.

Likewise the fourth entry shows that a cheque for £95.99 has been presented and cleared by the bank, representing payment of the British Telecom invoice. The DR entry on the bank statement means there would have been a CR entry on the cash account, which originally would have meant a DR entry to the Telephones account; not a Trade creditor as with Lyn's Haberdashery (a liability of the business) but an Expense account. You may wish to continue down the page and "create" your own accounts to cross reference to entries that you can likewise create on the bank statement, as indicated under the reference column and left blank for that purpose.

Now let us look at the last two entries on the statement.

Obviously nobody can estimate what interest if any will be earned over a period, because credit balances will fluctuate, as may interest rates. But interest must be accounted for within the business, by two entries, a DR to the cash account, (since it appears on the statement as a CR) and a corresponding CR entry to an "Interest Received " account. Since it is money coming into the business it must be included in either the Capital or Income categories. Obviously it is a class of Income, since it has been "earned" and not contributed. It will therefore appear in the Profit and Loss account.

The final entry, Bank Charges, is obviously an Expense of the business and will likewise appear in the Profit and Loss account. Since it appears as a DR on the bank statement it will appear in the Cashbook as a CR. Accordingly a corresponding DR entry will be entered into a "Bank Charges" account.

Turning to the internal books only, and ignoring the bank statement "control", here is a shorthand method of summarising these changes by reference to CRs and DRs, as a way of checking whether the entries are being made correctly.

Balance Sheet Entries

A DR entry in an account represents either

a) An increase in the value of an asset; or
b) A decrease in the value of a liability.

A CR entry in an account represents either

a) A decrease in the value of an asset; or
b) An increase in the value of a liability.

Profit and Loss Account Entries

Likewise a DR entry in an account represents either

a) An increase in the value of an Expense; or
b) A reduction in the value of an item of Income; or
c) Drawings.

A CR entry in an account represents either

a) An increase in the value of an item of Income; or
b) A reduction on the value of an Expense; or
c) Capital introduced.

Reference to one half of a table will reveal the other side, because of the rule that a CR in one account must also be represented by a corresponding DR in another.

Some further examples as reminders and practise:–

i) You pay by cheque an invoice rendered to the business for the purchase of Stationery.

   This is represented on the bank statement as a DR, when the cheque is cleared by the bank. Internally therefore a CR entry will be made on the Cash Account and a DR on the Stationery account (an Expense).

ii) An invoice is raised for a credit sale to a customer. So far there are no Cash account entries—nothing has been paid nor gone through the bank. A DR entry is made on the Debtors Account (the customer owes the value of the invoice to the business). A corresponding CR entry is made on the Sales account.

iii) The customer now pays the invoice by sending a cheque. A DR entry is made to the Cash account, which increases the value of the asset (i.e. Cash). A CR entry is made to the Debtors account (the liability) which reduces the balance on the account, because the customer no longer owes the money.

The golden rules to remember when discovering an error are firstly to identify what type of error it is and secondly whether the necessary adjustment requires a corresponding adjustment to another account as well.

4

THE TRIAL BALANCE

The Trial Balance is simply a listing of all the final balances on all the Nominal accounts, both CRs and DRs. It may be produced periodically, monthly or quarterly, as well as at the end of the financial year. As well as providing the raw material for the preparation of Final Accounts, it is a simple but effective way to check the arithmetical accuracy of the books.

A typical Trial Balance format might look as follows:–

		DRs	CRs
		£	£
*	Amounts owed by customers	3000	
	Cash at bank (Cash account)	2500	
	Petty Cash	60	
*	Administrative Expenses	1200	
	Computer Equipment	2000	
*	Furniture & Fittings	2000	
*	Sales		6800
	Creditors		460
	Capital		3500
		10760	10760

Balances marked by * are aggregate totals of all subsidiary accounts comprising that category.

i) Amounts owed by customers is another expression for Debtors. The figure shown could be made up from a large number of individual debtors, for which a subsidiary list would look as follows:

	DRs	CRs
J Smith	350	
C Brown	704	
F White	811	
etc.	x	
etc.	x	
etc.	x	
	3000	

Similarly

ii) Administrative expenses:

	DRs	CRs
Postage	98	
Telephones & Fax	246	
Stationery	321	
Printing	47	
Travel expenses	211	
etc.	x	
etc.	x	
etc.	x	
	1200	

Other accounts might also be shown as composites figures. The deciding factor will be the degree of complexity of the account. There is no absolute rule.

ii) The Sales account figure, taken from the Sales Ledger, will almost certainly represent the aggregate of a number of subsidiary sales accounts because it is simply best practise for control purposes to separate individual customer accounts.

These examples are used to illustrate the principles of the Trial Balance. So long as DR balances and CR balances are correctly identified as such then the process of extraction at the end of a period is straightforward. Should you need a reminder of the double entry system refer again to chapter 3. Remember that the Bank account acts as the "Control" account between the business and the bank, and that the Cash account acts as the "Control" account to all other internal accounts opened and maintained during the course of business.

There must be a corresponding DR on the Cash account for every CR entry shown on the Bank Statement and a corresponding CR entry on the Cash account for every DR on the Bank Statement.

For every CR entry on the Cash account there must be a corresponding DR entry on another internal account and for every DR entry on the Cash account a corresponding CR on another internal account — somewhere!

Therefore the total of all the CR balances must equal the total of all the DR balances.

If the DRs total on the Trial Balance equals the CRs total then you have "proved" that the accounts are accurate, is that not so?

Well, not necessarily!

The mathematical laws of probability suggest that when dealing with a large enough number of similar tasks, sooner or later an error will be made. This is a polite way of saying that nobody is perfect, and no book-keeper was ever perfect. There could be errors that are not revealed in a Trial Balance, which do not alter the fact that it balances.

Before looking at the more common types of error it is worth stating that as a starting point, if the Trial Balance does balance it is strong though not conclusive evidence that all the entries are correct.

Types of Error

The most common types of accounting error are as follows:

a) Errors of Omission. This describes the situation where a transaction is completely missing from the books, because not all the necessary entries have been made. This could arise because of oversight, or because there is no paperwork available to prompt the book-keeping.

b) Errors of Commission. Occur where entries are made, but in the wrong accounts, e.g. a sale of £35 is made to J Smith but entered in the account of B Smith.

c) Errors of Principle. Occur where entries are made in the wrong type of account, e.g. a prepayment expense (payment of an expense account in advance of the period to which it relates), which is an asset, is incorrectly entered as an accrual (an expense item for the current period for which no invoice has yet been received, which is a liability.

d) Compensating errors. Two or more errors which, taken together, cancel each other out. If in the illustration Petty Cash, £60, had been overlooked and omitted altogether from the list of DRs, and Creditors had been incorrectly totalled to read £400, not £460, the total DRs would still equal the total CRs, but this time £10700 in each case.

e) Errors of Original Entry. Occur where the original figure entered is incorrect on both the CR and the DR sides of different accounts, e.g. a credit sale of £132 to B Brown is entered in both the Sales account and the Debtors account as £123.

f) Reversal of entries. Occurs where the correct accounts are used but both entries are made on the wrong side, e.g. where the Sales account is debited and the Debtors account is credited, instead of vice versa.

Other possible errors include errors of addition, or only entering one half of a transaction, i.e. omitting to make either a CR or DR completely. Such errors would be revealed by a Trial Balance exercise unless compensatory errors had been made to conceal them.

Even though the Trial Balance is not a foolproof method of checking for accuracy it is the best one available for the small business proprietor using the double entry system, provided it is produced on a regular basis and with the necessary attention to detail. If the book-keeping has been accurate throughout the accounting period the total CRs on the books will equal or balance the total DRs, so because the system is self-balancing the scope for not finding errors is much reduced.

The golden rules to remember when discovering an error are firstly to identify what type of error it is and secondly whether the necessary adjustment requires a corresponding adjustment to another account as well.

5

THE FINAL ACCOUNTS

THE DISTINCTION BETWEEN CAPITAL AND REVENUE

All income received and all expenditure incurred by a business must be accounted for as either Capital or Revenue.

Capital

Simply put, Capital comprises the total of all kinds of wealth in a business used to produce Income. In the accounts, Capital must therefore be maintained intact, separate from other kinds of finance and clearly identified , showing reductions or increases.

Revenue

All other accounts record Revenue items, which are either income or expenditure, showing the day-to-day transactions of the business. As we have seen, the difference between income and expenditure is either a profit or a loss. Profits can be withdrawn from the business, while losses represent reductions to available Capital.

To successfully stay in business you have to sell sufficient goods/ services to generate:

i) enough revenue with which to carry on the business, i.e. cover the costs of running it; and

ii) a profit from which to draw out money to meet your personal living expenses; and

iii)perhaps enough additional profit to provide Capital to finance future growth, or to repay any capital loans from you and/or others to the business at the outset.

To successfully manage the business you need to know how all aspects of it relate to your sales, which is the underlying reason you keep accounts.

No matter how small or large your business is or becomes, you must know and monitor the following aspects of it;

i) The aggregate expenses of running it, over specific periods of time;
ii) The expenses in detail;
iii)How much money is tied up in stock and work-in-progress;
iv)What net profit is being made, period by period;
v) How much money is owed to the business;
vi)How much money is overdue for payment, and for how long;
vii)How much money is owed by the business and for how long.

All this information is revealed in the process of preparing a Trial Balance and in drawing up the Final Accounts.

Understanding what the books mean and keeping them up to date to reflect what has happened within it is vital for running it properly. Without well-kept books you cannot see where you've come from and if you don't know that you wont see where you are going. Incomplete or falsified books might fool you, but not your accountant nor the Tax authorities.

As we have seen, the two most important Final Accounts that either you or your accountant will prepare are:

i) The Profit and Loss Account; and
ii) The Balance Sheet.

Together these provide an historical record of the health and behaviour of the business, reduced to and expressed in terms of money.

THE PROFIT AND LOSS ACCOUNT

This subject was introduced in chapter 3 and, as the description implies it shows at a glance how much profit has been made, from a calculation of the total Income from business activities minus the total Expenditure incurred in running it.

There will be special characteristics in the layout chosen that reflect the uniqueness of your particular business, but in essence all P/L accounts follow the same basic format.

The Title Line is always set out as follows; the date chosen here is taken at random for illustration purposes.

The heads of text used are among the more common ones encountered in a small business.

DIANA'S FASHIONS

PROFIT & LOSS ACCOUNT FOR YEAR ENDED 31ST MARCH 199-

		£	£
	INCOME		
	Sales Proceeds	x	
Add:	Closing work in progress *	x	
Less:	Opening work in progress *	(x)	
	Bank Interest Receivable		x
Less:	EXPENDITURE		
	Administrative expenses	x	
	Salaries/wages *	x	
	Business Rates	x	
	Light & Heat *	x	
	Postage	x	
	Telephones	x	
	Stationery	x	
	etc.		
	etc.		
Add:	Accrued expenses*	x	
Less:	Prepaid Expenses*	(x)	
Add:	Bad Debts	x	
Add:	Depreciation of assets for year *	x	(x)
	NET PROFIT FOR YEAR		x

NOTES:

i) Closing-work-in-progress. At any one time you may have done work on orders which are not yet finished. This work therefore is "in progress" and represents income earned which has not yet been invoiced. It is recognised as such in the P/L account (and also shown in the Balance sheet as a Current asset). It has to be accounted for because ultimately you will be completing the work and receiving payment, so at the moment the accounts are produced (31st March), the business is "owed" the money.

Therefore you need to show Closing work-in-progress as an addition to Sales (CR) and show the same figure in the Balance Sheet as a Current Asset (DR).

ii) Opening-work-in-progress is the work that was in progress at the end of the previous accounting year and therefore must be deducted from Sales income for the year shown in these accounts. This is because it would have been invoiced and turned into Income during the year, or have become a bad debt and dealt with elsewhere in the accounts. If it were not deducted from this year's income it would have been included twice.

iii) Salaries/wages and Light/Heat could be further separated out if there were substantial sums involved.

iv) Accrued Expenses are the total of unpaid bills outstanding at 31st March. The figure represents expenses that have been incurred during the year but not yet paid. The appropriate adjustment in the accounts is to Increase the relevant expense, e.g. Telephones, in the P/L account (DR), and create a liability in the Balance Sheet (CR) to show that the sum is unpaid—as an "Accrued Expense".

v) Prepayments are expenses paid in advance of the period to which they relate, typically for such items as Insurance. Only those expenses incurred during the year can be charged to the P/L account. So any expense actually paid during this year but which relates to next year must be deducted from this year's expenses. The appropriate adjustment is to reduce the relevant expense, since it includes the amount prepaid (CR), and also create a debtor in the Balance Sheet (DR) under a separate heading of "Prepayments".

This is because if the business ceased to trade on 31st March (the Accounting Date), then any prepaid expense would have to be refunded to the business, so the prepayment is treated as a debtor.

vi) Bad Debts have been explained in chapter 3. In summary a bad debt is an amount owing to the business for work done/goods supplied but which has not been and is not going to be paid. It therefore becomes an expense or cost to the business and must be written off.

vii) Depreciation of assets. As explained in chapter 3 this is a subject best left to your accountant to advise upon. Technically it represents the proportion of the value of a fixed asset that has been "used up" in the current period to help produce the profit for the year.

viii) VAT is ignored for the purposes of drawing up final accounts. It is money that "passes through " a business but is independent of its operation, since it does not "belong" to the business.

ix) Figures shown as deductions in accounts are always expressed in brackets.

x) A calculation resulting from a deduction in the left hand column is extended one line lower and is shown in the centre column ; ditto in the centre column is extended one line lower and is shown in the right hand column , if 3 columns are used.

A further refinement to the accounts can arise if a fixed asset is sold during the course of a financial year. The question that has to be decided is this.

Was it sold at a loss, in which case the proceeds of sale will be shown as an Expense, or did the sale generate a profit, in which case that profit is shown as Income. Calculating a profit or loss from the sale of a fixed asset is a matter best left to your accountant.

It is quite possible for a loss to be made on the sale of an old asset even though cash or a cheque will be paid into the business!

It all depends upon the "Book value " of the asset at the time of sale, which again depends upon deducting the accumulated depreciation from its cost price. Suffice it to know that the sale proceeds must be accounted for in the P/L account.

No indication has been made in the illustration of taxation since the subject is beyond the scope of this book and to keep explanations as simple as possible. It should come as no surprise to learn that profits are taxed, after deducting all relevant allowances. The final accounts submitted to the Inland Revenue will normally accompany your personal Tax Return form, but again this is best left to your accountant.

In any event, as a sole trader, or in partnership with others, you still have to pay NI contributions. These are recorded in a separate column, if you use a Single Entry cashbook system, or in a NI account if you use a Double Entry system.

A different layout of the Profit and Loss account for a small manufacturing business might appear as follows:

BASH STREET METAL BASHERS

PROFIT & LOSS ACCOUNT FOR YEAR ENDED 31st MARCH 199-

		£
	TURNOVER	x
Less:	Cost of Sales	(x)
	=	GROSS PROFIT
Less:	EXPENSES	
	Distribution Costs	x
	Administrative expenses	x
	=	TRADING PROFIT

NOTES:

i) Turnover means Sales Revenue net of VAT.

ii) Cost of Sales is the total of all costs associated with making the products sold in the period. These would include raw materials costs; wages and salaries of workers; an appropriate proportion of production overheads including factory/workshop costs, but would exclude the costs of unsold production i.e. stock.

iii) Distribution costs and administrative expenses are self explanatory.

It is useful to remind ourselves once again that all the items in the P/L account are Nominal Accounts, as first mentioned in chapter 3, i.e. accounts in name only, since they do not relate to "Real" tangible assets nor to "Personal" accounts, for persons.

THE BALANCE SHEET

Together with the P/L account, the Balance Sheet sets out in summary form the financial position of the business at the close of the financial year.

Like the P/L account, various methods of presentation layout are possible, though usually a three or four column vertical form is used to show the broad categories of information, as illustrated later in the narrative.

The "Capital Employed" by a business is the term used to describe and explain the value of the capital that is used to generate the profit or loss, as calculated and shown on the P/L account. It is conventionally shown under that descriptive heading, below which are the various categories of Capital utilised.

The other half of the Balance Sheet is set out under the descriptive heading entitled "Employment of Capital". This shows the areas of the business where the capital is utilised, e.g. how much capital is represented by Fixed Assets, and by Current assets, and by Work-in-progress, etc. etc. Also shown is the money owed to the business and how much the business owes to its creditors.

The terminology used suggests that the total value of Capital Employed must equal the total value of the other half of the Balance Sheet equation, Employment of Capital. If this is not the case, then the Balance Sheet will not balance, which means that an error or series of errors has occurred in the calculations.

Errors could occur literally anywhere, in any account or a series of accounts.

Considering that the Balance Sheet is the culmination of a whole financial year's book-keeping, it is a timely reminder of the importance of regular and accurate book-keeping and the production of frequent trial balance exercises.

If for example monthly trial balances have been drawn down accurately for the first ten months of the financial year, then it follows that any errors must have occurred in the final two months. In most cases this will be so. But there remains one other area of potential error and that is the figure calculated for Profit or Loss for the year. This figure is carried forward from the P/L account to the Balance Sheet because it represents an addition to Capital Employed, if a profit, or a reduction to Capital Employed in the case of a Loss. If that figure is wrongly calculated then the Balance Sheet wont balance, so it is good practice to check it first.

As a matter of form it does not matter whether "Capital Employed" is set out before or after "Employment of Capital".

Either method of presentation is acceptable, although the more modern form is to show "Employment of Capital" first, followed by "Capital Employed".

This will be the format followed in our illustration. We will recall that the categories of account appearing in the Balance Sheet are the Assets and Liabilities of the business.

A) ASSETS.

These include all the items of value owned by the business, including what is owed to it. Each is shown in one of two categories as follows:

i) Fixed Assets. Those with a relatively long life which are used on a continuing basis in the activities of the business and are sometimes referred to as Tangible assets. They include freehold premises, the value of a leasehold, furniture, motor vehicles, machinery and equipment.

ii) Current Assets. These are Cash or other assets expected to be converted into cash in the near future. It is an accounting convention to show them in increasing order of "liquidity", i.e. the ease with which they are convertible into cash, the least liquid being shown first, as follows:

a) Closing Work-in-progress and/or Stock are the least liquid because you don't know when they will be converted into cash by sales.

b) Next comes Debtors (customers who have yet to pay for goods/services supplied), sometimes shown as Amounts due from Customers/Clients. From this sum will be deducted any amount assumed to be Bad Debts.

Note that if a "Bad Debt" does get paid later, an adjustment must be made in the subsequent year's Balance Sheet.

c) Next in order of liquidity will be payments made in advance, or Prepayments. Think about this from the "snap shot" viewpoint, which is what the Final Accounts represents. A payment made in advance is a kind of "loan" and a refund would be due should trading cease at the end of the accounting period.

Therefore it is an asset. Prepayments occur because financial periods for your insurers, for example, do not necessarily coincide with the financial year of the business, so overlap payments often occur if such payments are required in advance.

d) Next in order of liquidity is Cash at the bank.

e) Finally the most liquid of all assets is Cash in hand, represented by Petty Cash, accounting for which will be dealt with in chapter 6.

B) LIABILITIES

From the aggregate total of Fixed and Current assets must be deducted the total Liabilities of the business at the "snap shot" date, i.e. the monies owed by the business.

i) **Current Liabilities**. Are those debts which fall to be paid within the coming 12 months. These include:

a) Bank Overdrafts

b) Trade Creditors

c) Outstanding expenses. These are running costs not yet paid, otherwise known as Accruals or Accrued expenses.

ii) **Long term Liabilities. Those** debts falling due for settlement 12 months or more after the date of the Balance Sheet. Such liabilities are usually Long Term loans but exclude bank overdrafts, which can be called in at short notice at any time.

A typical Balance Sheet layout looks as follows:

BALANCE SHEET AS AT 31st MARCH 199-

EMPLOYMENT OF CAPITAL

	£	£	£
FIXED ASSETS			
Land and buildings at cost			x
Fixtures & Fittings at cost		x	
Less: Accumulated Depreciation		(x)	
			x
Motor Vehicles at cost		x	
Less: Accumulated Depreciation		(x)	
			x
			x

	£	£	£
CURRENT ASSETS			
Closing work-in-progress		x	
Debtors (owed by customers)	x		
Less: Provision for doubtful debts	(x)		
		x	
Prepayments		x	
Cash at Bank		x	
Petty Cash		x	
		x	
LESS: CURRENT LIABILITIES			
Bank Overdraft	x		
Creditors	x		
Accrued Expenses	x		
		(x)	
NET CURRENT ASSETS			x
LESS: LONG TERM LIABILITIES			
Bank loan			(x)
			x
REPRESENTED BY			
Capital as at 1st April (same year)			x
Add: Net Profit for year			x
			x
Less: Drawings from the business			(x)
			x

Notes:

i) Deductions are again always shown in brackets;

ii) A calculation resulting from a deduction in the left hand column is extended one line lower and shown in the centre column; ditto in the centre column is extended one line lower and shown in the far right hand column.

Another purpose of the Balance Sheet is to provide a basis for valuing the business as an entity. Taken literally, a Balance Sheet is a sheet of the balances taken from the double entry system of book-keeping at the end of a financial year.

But the values shown are probably not what the business is worth. This value would reflect the subjective judgment of a potential buyer, considering his/her estimation of the market value, perhaps building in an allowance for "goodwill", i.e. the value attaching to the name and reputation of the business. Also the asset valuation method used by a buyer is normally based on present market values, not the historical cost of the assets used in arriving at the book values.

As we have seen, the principle of Double Entry provides that in the Balance Sheet the total Assets must equal the total Capital.

The total Capital is another way of describing the sources of finance used in a business, which is another way of describing what is owed by the business to those providers of the finance.

Let us examine the sources of finance available to a business. These consist of:

a) Current liabilities owed to creditors, i.e. debts due for settlement within 12 months (money owed to creditors does not belong to the business but is used by it); and

b) Long term liabilities, i.e. debts due for settlement 12 months or more after the end of the financial year; and

c) Capital provided by the owner(s) of the business. Capital represents your personal financial interest, i.e. what the business owes you.

The logic of the Double Entry system dictates that:

* An increase/decrease in the value of an asset must be matched by either

  i) An increase/decrease in a Source of Finance (a liability);

  or

  ii) An increase/ decrease in the value of another asset.

* An increase/decrease in a Source of Finance must be matched by either

  i) An increase/decrease in the value of an asset

  or

  ii) An increase/decrease in another Source of Finance.

Finally, remember that a Balance Sheet can be struck at any time, not just at the year end, though generally speaking it is only left until then.

6

ACCOUNTING FOR PETTY CASH

Small Cash payments will need to be made in the day-to-day course of business. Accordingly it is necessary to record these payments separately from the main cash account because:

i) they are made in cash;

ii) being small sums it is easier to lose track of how much has been spent and on what;

iii) they are business costs like any made by cheque and must be accounted for as expenses.

A word of warning. If cash sales are made in the course of business **DO NOT** account for them in the petty cash accounts. Sales are **NOT** to be confused with minor expenses.

Mixing the two kinds of cash is not uncommon in cash-based businesses, but it is a fundamental error of principle and practice.

Always record petty cash expenditure as it is incurred, preferably by the use of pre-printed vouchers. You also need a ready-ruled

Petty cash accounts book to compile the account from the vouchers. Both can be bought from your business stationers.

In the normal course of events you always carry some cash with you, going about your personal daily affairs. Sometimes you will be going about the affairs of the business at the same time and will need to distinguish the following occasions when you spend cash:

A) ON THE BUSINESS PREMISES

From time to time you will need postage stamps, biro pens, packets of envelopes, tea, milk, coffee, etc. and cash can be used from your Petty cash box for these purchases. Even if you use your own money you must still record the purchase on a voucher and re-imburse yourself from the petty cash box, because the business owes that money to you.

B) ON YOUR TRAVELS

All money spent by you in the course of business is a legitimate business expense, because it comes from business funds and therefore "belongs" to the business, not to you personally.

Get into the habit of asking for receipts for small sums spent and staple each receipt to a voucher. With or without receipts, total up the sum spent, on a weekly basis, and write a business account cheque to yourself for the amount expended from your personal funds.

Typically purchases will be for such items as petrol, parking meters, railway tickets, mini-cab fares and perhaps telephone calls made out of the office, e.g. from home. Some of these examples will generate receipts, some not. In all case, if you are registered for VAT (see chapter 7) you must record the VAT separately, because it will be recoverable. (Remember that stamps and food items do not carry VAT).

Petty Cash Exercise for Helen (t/a Helen's Fashions)

At the end of a busy week Helen, (trading as Helen's Fashions) took the following receipts for various purchases from her bag and from the glove compartment of her car:

	£
Petrol	15.20
Buttons	6.75
Lunch (with Susan Jones)	27.75
Phone Cards	8.00
Rail Ticket	14.30

Her diary for that week showed that Helen had spent further small sums without obtaining receipts:

Parking meters	3.50
Telephone calls (coins)	1.20
Trade Newspaper	2.60
Tea, sugar, milk	4.95
Mini-cab fares	6.00

Notes:

i) Helen is to be commended for being a methodical and disciplined businesswoman.

ii) Lunch expenses with Susan Jones. Business entertainment expenses are not tax deductible unless Helen can prove to the Inland Revenue that they led to her obtaining business outside the U.K.

If the lunch did lead to an export deal she has a prima facie case for claiming it as an allowable business expense.

An exception arises in the provision of Xmas lunches/drinks for employees, where the Inland Revenue allow a modest sum for the "Xmas bash". Check the current limits with your accountant since Tax legislation changes every year.

How much Petty cash should be kept in the business?

By implication (and for security purposes), such sums should be small, to cover say 1-2 weeks average weekly spend.

The recording system

The most common form of Petty Cash control is called the Imprest System, which works in the following way.

Having decided on, say, £50 as a comfortable and realistic "float", draw this sum from the business bank account by cheque. During week 1 assume say £38.50 is spent, leaving £11.50 in the box.

At the start of week 2, draw out by business cheque a further sum of £38.50, bringing the petty cash float back up to £50.

The Imprest system can be checked at any time. Cash in hand plus the amount detailed on petty cash vouchers (for cash spent) for the period should always total £50.

As mentioned, a pre-printed Petty Cash book is the most sensible method for permanently recording how much has been spent and on what. Analysis columns will enable you to categorise expenses in the same way that major expenses are detailed in the Analysed Cashbook.

The following example would be spread across one page of the book:

Column	1	2	3	4	5
	Receipts	Folio	Date	Voucher	Total Spent
	£				£
	50.00	CB4		17	22.00

Column	6	7	8	9	10
	VAT	Postage	Petrol	Parking	Refresh- ments
		2.00			
		3.00			
			5.00		
				7.00	
					5.00

5.00 5.00 7.00 5.00

Column	1	2
	Receipts	Folio
	22.00	CB5

Notes:

i) Folio. Refers to the page number of the Cashbook or Cash Account that records the cash withdrawn for petty cash and is a cross-reference to that main account.

ii) The second drawing is the second receipt into the float = £22. This represents the amount of cash "reimbursed" to the Petty Cash, to bring the total back up to £50, which is carried down to the next page in the petty cash book for the following month, which naturally is the new opening balance.

As illustrated, the recording method is "self-contained", because the folio entry connects the Petty cash account with the main accounting procedures of the business - either the Cashbook or the Cash account.

For the sake of brevity it has been assumed no VAT has been paid on the purchases.

If you intend to use the Double entry system you will need to complete the double entry of expenses and receipts.

As we already know the Bank Statement will show a DR entry for the cash withdrawn. Therefore the Cash Account will record a CR as the corresponding entry. Therefore the Petty Cash Receipt entries will represent the DR entries of the internal Accounting system. The corresponding CR entries are therefore the expenses columns in the Petty Cash book, summarised first in the Totals column.

To finalise the double entry, add up each expense column and enter this sum as a DR on the relevant "main" account. So for example the amount for petrol can be DR-ed to the Travel Expenses Account, and likewise for all other petty cash disbursements.

7

ACCOUNTING FOR VAT

A fully comprehensive guide to the complexities of the VAT system is beyond the scope of this book and only a brief outline will be provided. Suffice it to say that if you are registered for VAT with HM C&E then you are liable to account to that authority for VAT passing through your books. In effect you are an unpaid tax collector.

Your local VAT office will advise you on all VAT matters and enquiries regarding VAT administration. Do not neglect to seek advice from C&E and/or your accountant before you commence business, because:

a) the best advice will depend upon the circumstances of your business; and

b) you will not be excused by HM Customs & Excise for failing to get advice. The C&E will presume you have been so advised on how the system works and what you have to do; and

c) the system is complex.

THE VAT SYSTEM

Value Added Tax is defined as the tax chargeable on the supply of goods or services, where the supply is a taxable supply and made by a taxable person in the course of business carried on by him/her. The taxable person is s/he who is liable to account to HM C&E for the amount of tax charged on the supply of goods/services.

A "BUSINESS"

When are you in business and when are you not?

"Business" can have a very wide meaning and includes the way in which self-employed individuals earn income by way of trade, vocation or profession.

HM C&E define business as "any continuing activity which is mainly concerned with making supplies to other persons for a consideration".

Supply of Goods

This means a supply that transfers the exclusive ownership of the goods to someone else.

Supply of Services

This means doing something (except supplying goods), and receiving in return what the law calls a "consideration". This means any kind of payment – monetary or otherwise, and includes something which is also a supply. So a "consideration" to the business in return for the business making a supply includes anything given to cover the costs of making the supply.

Taxable Supply

This means any supply of goods/services except an exempt supply. Exempt supplies are listed in Schedule 6 of the VAT Act 1983 and include insurance, financial and postal services, and health services.

Taxable supplies are of two kinds:

i) Those chargeable at the Standard rate (currently 17.5%).

ii) Those chargeable at a zero rate. Zero rated supplies include water, books and periodicals, and food not consumed on premises but which is sold for outside consumption.

Exempt and Zero-rated supplies are similar because no VAT is actually charged in either case to a customer.

However, you must be aware of the crucial difference between the two because only a registered business that makes a Taxable supply can reclaim VAT paid for supplies to that business.

Zero rated supplies are taxable supplies. If your business makes Zero rated supplies it is a "Taxable Person" for VAT purposes. This means that VAT can be claimed back on purchases made by a business that is zero rated, if it is registered.

Exempt supplies are **not** taxable supplies. If your business only makes Exempt supplies it is not a "Taxable Person" for VAT purposes and therefore VAT paid on purchases by the business cannot be reclaimed from HM C&E.

There are special and complex rules about partial exemption applicable to suppliers of exempt goods/services (health operations, financial services and a few others). If you believe your business might qualify then contact your local VAT office. Briefly the size, type and level of business determine whether your business qualifies for partial exemption.

It should be clear by now that VAT can apply to your business even if the turnover is quite modest, because it is inevitable that

VAT is going to be paid on purchases, regardless of whether it is charged on sales.

Discounts on Taxable Supplies

If you intend to offer discounts on products or services, as many businesses do, you need to know the VAT position on this kind of sale.

There are two kinds of discount in operation in business.

a) An unconditional discount to a customer naturally means that s/he will pay the asking price less the discount. VAT is charged on the lower price because that is the asking price, the one the buyer will accept.

b) A conditional discount is one where a lower price will operate provided that the buyer pays promptly within a specified discount period, e.g. 14 days. In this case VAT is charged on the lower, discounted sum even if the customer does not pay within the specified discount period.

The tax value of the supply is the value of what is provided on which VAT is charged, because the lower sum will be at least the minimum amount paid for the purchase, assuming that the buyer takes advantage of the discounted price.

Time of Supply

The time at which a supply is made is known as the Tax Point. It is important because it begins the period at the end of which a taxable business becomes liable to account for tax charged on a taxable supply.

Generally the Tax Point for the sale of goods is when the goods are given over to the purchaser, which of course may not be when they are paid for, as in a credit sale.

The Tax Point for services is when the services are completed, which again may not be the same time as when they are paid for.

The most important exceptions are:

i) If a tax invoice is issued within 14 days after the basic tax point, the invoice date will be the tax point for the purpose of fixing the beginning of the quarterly period of account in which the VAT on it becomes liable for payment to HM C&E, unless a longer period is agreed.

ii) If payment is received, or a tax invoice rendered before the basic tax point arises, then the supply will be treated as occurring at the date the payment was made, or the date the invoice was rendered.

REGISTRATION

A) Compulsory

If you anticipate that the sales income of the business in the current trading year will reach the threshold level prescribed by law (currently £46000 for the tax year 1995-96), you must contact your local VAT office and inform them that the business is liable for registration for VAT.

Upon registration the business will be allotted a unique Registration number, which must be shown on all business stationery.

VAT must then be charged on all sales the business makes, whether on credit or for cash, at the prescribed rate, except on those goods/services which are either zero rated or exempt.

This is called the Output Tax.

The VAT paid by the business on purchases of materials etc. is called the Input tax.

HM C&E must be paid the amount of VAT charged by the business on sales (**whether collected within the relevant quarter**

or not) minus the VAT paid by the business on its purchases. This is normally done at the end of each quarter, though a longer time period can sometimes be negotiated.

Retail businesses, i.e. those selling to the public, do not need to render VAT invoices unless a buyer requests one.

HM C&E publish a number of leaflets and notices explaining in great detail all you need to know about VAT and your business, as a sole trader, partnership or limited company.

Among the most important are:

i) VAT Notice 700: The VAT Guide. In fact a booklet of more than 140 pages.

ii) "Should I register for VAT?". This Guide is vital because HM C&E will impose financial penalties for failure to register when you should and also for late payments.

If you are fairly confident that within the next 30 days your taxable turnover for the past 12 months will exceed the threshold limit, then you must inform HM C&E.

iii) "Filling in your VAT Return". A useful guide on what format to adopt and how to present VAT Return forms.

If you believe that you are not obliged to register, because turnover will remain below the threshold, you should still consider the issue carefully. There are circumstances when you can reclaim VAT incurred before registration, if you then register at a later date.

For example, VAT paid on vans (but not cars) and stock can later be reclaimed, disregarding the time of purchase, so long as the items are for business use. Of course you must produce VAT invoices to evidence the amount reclaimed.

If you engage the services of either solicitors or estate agents to set up the business, then VAT on their fee invoices can be reclaimed if they were incurred up to 6 months before the business was registered.

b) Voluntary

Compulsory registration arises simply because of the proximity of your turnover to the threshold level.

As an alternative you may want to consider voluntary registration, even if your turnover is substantially below the threshold level for compulsory registration.

The advantage is of course that Input tax paid on purchases subject to VAT can then be reclaimed.

The disadvantage is that VAT will have to be charged on the taxable supplies made by the business, which could well affect the competitiveness of your products/services. If competitors are not charging VAT and you are this might present a serious problem.

If the business is not registered, compulsorily or voluntarily, then it will have to bear the incidence of Input tax paid. You will have to consider whether the business can absorb this cost or whether you need to raise the selling prices.

TAX INVOICES

A) Inputs to the Business

Once registered tax invoices are important because they evidence your right to recover Input tax on supplies made to the business by a supplier who is also registered. Without tax invoices you will not be able to claim a deduction of the VAT paid.

B) Outputs of the Business

If you have registered the business then you are compelled to charge VAT on sales, whether on credit or for cash.

Furthermore, tax invoices can only be raised if the business is VAT registered, and not otherwise.

As a matter of good business practice it is best to quote a VAT-inclusive price to customers. The current rate is significantly high and could have a serious impact on the cash flows of your own business and that of your suppliers, because most registered persons and businesses are locked in to the quarterly Return cycle.

Assuming the business is registered, and is therefore a taxable person, then within 30 days of making a physical taxable supply, the customer must be provided with a tax invoice.

Every Tax Invoice must by law state the following particulars:–

a) An invoice number, for identification purposes

b) The date of the supply, i.e. the tax point

c) The name, address and VAT registration number of the business

d) The name and address of the person to whom the sale has been made

e) The kind of supply that has been made, e.g. sale, hire

f) An adequate description of the goods or services supplied

g) The precise quantity of goods supplied or the extent of the services provided and separate amounts payable under each heading

h) The total amount payable and a breakdown of separate amounts against each item, if more than one

i) Details of any discount allowable for prompt cash payment

j) The rate of tax applicable and the amount of tax charged.

An exception applies to the "bottom line" value of a tax invoice if the VAT inclusive total is less than £100.00. If this is so you don't need to show VAT as a separate calculation but can instead show the one grossed-up sum on an abbreviated tax invoice.

It is important to get all this information correct on all Output invoices and also to check that it is right on Input invoices.

If upon inspection invoices do not satisfy HM C&E's requirements then you put at risk your ability to reclaim Input tax. Bear in mind that HM C&E have authority to inspect all your books and records relating to VAT at any time, with or without your co-operation.

An additional aid to VAT invoice monitoring is a simple Invoice book, listing all invoices raised in number sequence and with separate analysis columns providing for arithmetic calculation of Output VAT and net sales.

TAX COLLECTION

As noted previously, accounting for VAT is almost always with reference to quarterly accounting periods. With permission from HM C&E you may want to opt for an annual accounting scheme, where one Tax Return is made at the end of the year and the tax liability paid by Direct Debit in 9 monthly instalments of amounts agreed with the C&E.

Within one month after the end of a tax quarter, a completed Return Form and a cheque for the tax due must be sent to HM C&E. Penalties are levied for late payment.

The Statutory Return form provided by your local VAT office must detail the amount payable and how that sum has been calculated i.e. the total output tax charged less the total input tax deductible. The Return must also detail the VAT-exclusive values of all sales and purchases made and incurred. The leaflet accompanying the form shows you exactly how to set this information out.

Bad Debt Relief

As noted previously, it is possible that your business will incur a bad debt from time to time. The amount to be written off can include VAT if the invoice raised was a VAT invoice.

Relief can be claimed for the VAT element of a bad debt which is more than 6 months old and has been written-off in your accounts. If the debt is subsequently paid then naturally you must refund the VAT portion of the debt, whether recovered in whole or in part.

ACCOUNTING FOR VAT IN YOUR BOOKS

You are required to keep records of all taxable supplies and receipts of taxable goods and services made in the course of business. This includes standard, zero rated and exempt supplies.

If your methods of keeping these records create problems for HM C&E in any audit exercise carried out they have power to direct necessary changes to your procedures.

All VAT records must be kept for 6 years and can only be disposed of before 6 years with the permission of HM C&E.

We have already examined how to highlight the VAT element in your books of account.

a) The Single Entry Analysed Cashbook System

On both the Receipts side and the Payments side of the Cashbook identify the VAT element and the net amount by using separate analysis columns for each.

b) The Double Entry Cash Account System

A separate VAT/HM C&E account is maintained, as for any other type of account, to record movements of VAT.

8

Bank Reconciliations

The purpose of bank reconciliations is to match what the bank statement shows as being in the business bank account at the end of an accounting period (usually a month), to what your books of account show as the position. In other words a reconciliation exercise of the external control of the business to the internal control system, i.e. the Cashbook or the Cash Account.

It is essential to conduct bank reconciliation exercises on a regular basis because it is an effective way

i) to assess the accuracy of your book-keeping; and

ii) to compare the financial state of the business with an external reference, which operates to monitor the behaviour of the business.

Discrepancies between the monthly closing balances of the cashbook/cash account and the bank statement will inevitably occur because of the time lags in the processing and recording of monies paid in to the bank.

A bank reconciliation statement should be set out methodically and follow a simple system of recording discrepancies. The reconciliation statement should start with the balance according to the bank statement. Adjustments are then made by listing all the items which have not been entered in either set of books at the relevant date. A balance is then struck at the end of this arithmetic exercise showing the true position of the account, both internal and external balances being the same.

The reasons for the time lags that produce the overall discrepancy between the two accounts include the following:

i) Cheques may have been drawn and the payments entered in the appropriate internal books or on the payments side of the cashbook, but not yet cleared through the banking system. Cheques can take between 3 to 5 working days to clear the system, depending on whether they are drawn on one of the four clearing banks, or on a smaller bank or Building Society account.

   If a cheque drawn on your business account does not appear on the bank statement it is "unpresented".
   The appropriate adjustment is to add the payment-out to the DR side of the bank statement, thus decreasing the balance if in credit, or increasing an overdraft, if shown.

ii) Receipts recorded in your books may have been too recent to have been cleared by the bank. Such cheques may have been banked at a different branch to your own, or they may reflect cash/cheques received but not yet banked.
   The appropriate adjustment is to add the receipts to the CR side of the bank statement, thus increasing the balance if in credit or decreasing an overdraft, if shown.

iii) DR items may appear on the bank statement but not in the cashbook. Examples include:

a) Bank charges debited automatically by the bank for operating the account;
b) Standing Order payments - regular payments to the credit of others and paid by the bank on your instructions e.g. business rates;
c) Direct debits - charges automatically made on the account by another person, though with your authority e.g. insurance premiums.
The appropriate adjustments for all of these is the same as in (i) above. Reduce the balance in the cashbook/cash account by way of a CR entry or an entry in the payments side of the analysed cashbook.

iv) CR items may appear on the bank statement but not in the cashbook/cash account. This can happen if a debtor pays one of your invoices by instructing his/her bank to credit your bank, rather than posting the cheque to you.
The appropriate adjustment is the same as in (ii) above. Increase the balance in the cashbook/cash account by way of a DR entry.

v) It is uncommon but not unknown for banks to make errors in preparing bank statements. Such errors will become apparent in the process of reconciliation.

vi) It is likewise not unknown for book-keepers to make errors of the kinds explained earlier. Again these will be revealed in the reconciliation process.

Before drawing up the reconciliation statement the following steps are advisable.

- First tick off all payments and receipts in the cashbook/cash account with all the corresponding items on the bank statement.
- Then enter into the cashbook/cash account all bank charges, direct debits, standing orders and interest receipts and tick off those.

Any remaining unticked items must therefore be unpresented cheques or late credits. Make a list of each and draw up a reconciliation statement in the following format, using the bank statement as the "control" account.

RECONCILIATION STATEMENT AS AT (last day of month)

		£	£
	Closing Balance as per Bank Statement		x
Less:	Unpresented cheques	x	
		x	(x)
			x
Add:	Late credits	x	
		x	x
Balance as per adjusted Cashbook			x

This illustrates the situation where the bank statement shows a CR closing balance, that is the account is in credit.

If the closing balance shows an overdraft then to calculate the true position the procedure shown above must be reversed.

Starting with a DR balance at the bank as the closing balance, unpresented cheques must be added, since they will increase the DR figure. Likewise, late credits must be subtracted since they reduce the amount owed to the bank.

The format used can be varied, but so long as the principles are understood and applied then the two balances should be reconciled with little difficulty.

9

Accounts for Small Partnerships

It is not difficult to form a partnership in order to conduct a business activity. All that is required is to meet the definition of a partnership stated in Section 1 of The Partnership Act 1890: " A partnership is the relation which subsists between persons carrying on a business in common with a view of profit".

A partnership exists if there is evidence that a person receives a share of the net profits of a business enterprise. Even a person who plays no active role can be a partner - a "sleeping partner" - if they receive a share of the profit after tax. No formal written document or Partnership Agreement/Deed is required to form a partnership.

The importance of knowing whether you are trading in a partnership lies in the area of liability for debts.

In law each and every partner is liable for all the debts of a firm "without limit".

If things go wrong, any one partner cannot successfully argue that the other partners are liable for "fair shares".

"Without limit" means just that. Liability is unlimited and includes all personal assets owned outside of the business, including homes.

According to section 9 of the Partnership Act 1890: " Every Partner in a firm is liable with the other partners for all debts and obligations of the firm while he was a partner".

This is known as Joint and Several liability. This provision operates even if there is a written Partnership Agreement, which may provide for a right of contribution from the other partners. If though, on a dissolution, for any reason, the other partners cannot pay, then there is no protection from section 9.

There can be (and would be) agreement about shares of profits in a Partnership Agreement, but any agreement about a share of debts is unenforceable at law. A creditor deciding to sue a Partnership will usually sue each and every partner for the full sum at issue.

Broadly speaking there are two situations where a Partnership comes into being:

a) where a sole trader joins with someone else and by agreement, written or otherwise, changes his/her personal business status to that of a partner in a firm; or
b) where 2 or more persons (the maximum prescribed by law for most kind of business is 20), decide at the outset to enter into a business relationship in the form of a partnership.

The most important constraint on either starting a partnership or expanding a sole proprietorship into one will be the availability of capital to finance the endeavour.

In either case finance is provided by the partners in the form of their capital contribution. This can be with their own money, and/or money that they borrow for the purpose and/or their personal property. Money borrowed can be from any source – a bank, a relative, a friend or even from a business partner.

PROPERTY USED IN A PARTNERSHIP

Confusion sometimes arises over what constitutes partnership property and what is the personal property of partners.

Two kinds of property might be used in a partnership, as follows:

i) Property owned by the partnership as such. This is property paid for from partnership funds and clearly identified as being for the exclusive benefit of the firm; and

ii) Property owned personally by a partner but which is used by the partnership for partnership business.

Sometimes the distinction is obvious, sometimes not. It has to be made though because:

i) partnership property has to be dealt with when drawing up the final accounts of the partnership;

ii) if one partner contributes as capital say, office or workshop premises, who then is to pay business rates?

iii) in such a case will the partnership be charged rent by the owning partner?

For the avoidance of doubt these questions are best considered before business commences and decisions about them included in a formal, written Partnership Agreement. This would also include itemised schedules of both kinds of property used in the firm. The best advice is to instruct a solicitor to draw up the Partnership Agreement to reflect the intentions of all prospective partners, especially if one or more is to allow personal assets to be used by the business.

In the absence of an express written Agreement, an agreement about partnership property can be inferred in disputed cases from the partners' course of dealing by a Judge in Court proceedings, based on evidence of how business is usually conducted and by whom.

However, an Agreement will not normally be implied just because the partners want it to be implied. A Court will require evidence and infer by reference to the provisions of the Partnership Act. This legislation will be applied to the activities of the partnership regardless of what partners may or may not have agreed, or what they thought had been agreed between them. Hence the advantage of a written Agreement, because as in other forms of business arrangement, a Partnership is a legal entity separate from the individuals carrying on the business of the firm.

THE PARTNERSHIP AGREEMENT

Financial and accounting matters that should be dealt with in a Partnership Agreement include:

a) How much start-up Capital each partner is to contribute;

b) Whether or not Interest is to be paid on Capital contributions before profits are distributed and if so at what annual rate;

c) The Profit/Loss sharing ratio to be applied for each partner;

d) Whether Interest is to be charged on Drawings that exceed an agreed level and if so at what rate;

e) Whether or not Salaries are to be paid, to whom and on what basis.

If no written Partnership Agreement has been entered into and if one cannot be implied by reference to documents or inferred from a course of dealing, then Section 24 of the Partnership Act will operate to determine these questions by law, as follows:

a) No Interest will be paid on original Capital contributions.

b) Further Capital contributions in excess of that originally brought into the partnership will earn Interest at a rate of 5% p.a.

c) Profits and losses will be apportioned in equal shares.

d) No Interest can be charged on drawings.

e) No salaries can be paid.

PARTNERSHIP ACCOUNTING MATTERS

Let us examine these issues in more detail.

a) Profit Sharing Ratios

Because capital contributions are determined at the start of business and may very well be in unequal shares, it does not automatically follow that profit shares have to reflect the same proportions.

Suppose for example, in the 2 partner firm of Green & White, Green contributed 80% of the Capital sum of £100,000 and White the remaining 20%.

Green might be content with a 50%–50% share of the profits. Alternatively he may insist on a more equitable distribution to reflect the greater personal risk implied by his greater capital contribution.

b) Interest on Capital

As another alternative he might agree to a 50%–50% profit share only if Interest is paid on capital before profits are shared. Interest in this case can be seen as the equivalent of a fixed profit share for the use of Capital contributed.

In reality of course precise divisions are a matter of agreement and are best negotiated to reflect notions of equity, risk and anticipated profitability.

Let us refer again to our example, using the same Capital contribution of 80%–20% and a 50%–50% share of profits. Given the substantial disparity between capital contributions, Green would no doubt insist that Interest on capital be paid before profits are distributed, so that his total income from the firm more closely reflects his overall contribution.

see opposite

On this basis, Green's total share of the £30,000 profit is 60%, with White getting the remaining 40%.

There may however be further considerations in reaching agreement, including different contributions of time, effort and skills by the partners to the firm.

Suppose the firm is in the business of making-up and selling dresses.

Green's capital contribution might be in the form of business premises, office equipment and a delivery van. He collects materials from the firm's suppliers and delivers finished dresses to customers. He also handles the administration and keeps the books. His working week is 3 days. Sometimes he acts as a salesman to get in new business. He cannot make dresses.

White is a first-class dressmaker. Her initial Capital contribution consists of a large supply of dress-making materials and cutting & sewing machines. She works 5 days a week, hates administration, does not drive and is just too busy to attend to any paperwork.

Such scenarios are not uncommon in small partnerships.

In such circumstances, how do they share the total profit in a way that they both feel is equitable and therefore workable?

We can see how this looks below, assuming:–

(i) net profit for the year of £30,000;

(ii)Interest on capital to be paid at 10% p.a.:

		£	£
1. Net profit for year			30,000
2. Capital contribution:			
	Green	80,000	
	White	20,000	
3. Interest on Capital at 10% p.a.:			
	Green 80,000 x 10% =	8,000	
	White 20,000 x 10% =	2,000	(10,000)
	Remaining profit =		20,000
4. Share of remaining Profit:	Green 50%		10,000
	White 50%		10,000
5. Total Income:			
Green		8,000 Interest	
		1,000 Remaining profit share	
		18,000	
White		2,000 Interest	
		10,000 Remaining profit share	
		12,000	

c) Salary Payments

As well as paying Interest on capital and agreeing a remaining-profit sharing ratio, a further way to balance unequal contributions is to pay a salary to one or both partners before the division of residual profit. A salary therefore would represent a fixed payment out of profit, paid to reflect additional contributions of time, expertise etc.

Thus a salary is an expense of the business, paid like salaries to employees and is not the same as drawings.

In our example White may argue that she should be paid a sum by way of salary, to compensate for the extra 2 days per week she works for the firm, and because the firm's prosperity rests more on her dress-making expertise, rather than on Green's administrative and driving skills.

Again, any salary would be paid out of profits before the division of the remainder according to the profit sharing ratio.

Returning to our example, and assuming White is paid a salary of £6000:

		£	£
1. Net profit for year:			30,000
2. Capital contribution:			
	Green 80,000		
	White 20,000		
3. Interest on Capital at 10% p.a.:			
	Green 80,000 x 10% =	8,000	
	White 20,000 x 10% =	2,000	(10,000)
	Remaining Profit =		20,000

		£
4. Salaries:		
Green NIL		
White 6,000		(6,000)
Remaining Profit =		14,000

5. Share of remaining Profit:		
Green	7,000	
White	7,000	
		14,000

6. Total Income:

Source	Green	White	Profit £ 30,000
	£	£	
Interest on Capital	8,000	2,000	10,000
Salaries	NIL	6,000	6,000
Share of Profit	7,000	7,000	14,000
	15,000	15,000	30,000

Equality at last!

d) Interest on Drawings-down of Profits

To maintain the amount of cash in the business and inhibit drawings beyond agreed limits, a useful discipline to consider is to charge interest on excess drawings. A profligate partner would be penalised by having to repay interest, as well as possibly earning interest on capital at the same time.

Day to Day Accounting for a Small Partnership

If the business is small enough and the volume of transactions is manageable, then an Analysed Cashbook system can be used just as easily as for a sole proprietorship.

On the (right hand) Expenses side of the book, each partner can be identified by using a separate column for each individual's "Drawings". Alternatively, the book-keeper can use one Drawings column and indicate by name each partner making a drawing-out.

In a firm using the Double Entry system of book-keeping, the system operates in exactly the same way for a partnership as for a sole proprietorship.

Separate accounts are kept for each partner, to record transactions over the accounting period, in exactly the same way as for all other accounts.

Capital accounts would record initial contributions, any Interest earned, and any share of remaining profit "capitalised", i.e. "converted" into capital and retained in the business by the relevant partner. Following a capitalisation there would no doubt be a revision of the interest rate to be applied, should there appear too great a disparity in the adjusted capital contributions and allowance for this should be made in the Agreement.

Partners' Income from all sources – profit share, salary and/or drawings and Interest on capital – is best dealt with collectively in a single Current Account, one for each partner, and must not be aggregated with Capital.

FIXED AND CURRENT CAPITAL EXPLAINED

It is important to understand this distinction, to avoid "mixing" the two categories during the process of book-keeping.

Finance (that is money or money's worth), which will be used in a partnership originates from one or more of 4 possible sources:

a) Capital funds contributed by the owners at the start-up and possibly at later dates.

b) Loans from lending Institutions, from partners or other sources.

c) Credit extended by the firm for goods and services supplied to customers but which has not yet been paid to the business, i.e. Debtors.

d) Money generated from business activities, i.e. cash at the bank.

Finance from whatever source is used for the purpose of acquiring assets, i.e. something owned that confers a future economic benefit expressed in terms of money.

Capital Assets are classified as either Fixed or Current, according to Accounting Conventions.

Fixed assets include Land & Buildings (Freehold or Leasehold); Plant & Machinery; Furniture & Fixtures; Equipment; Vehicles.

As a guide, Fixed Assets are those acquired to facilitate the process of income generation over the long term, i.e. a period of more than one year, and not held for resale.

Current assets are those held with the purpose of conversion into cash in the short term i.e. less than one year. Examples include debtors; work-in-progress; raw materials and stock.

In short, whether an asset is fixed or current ultimately depends upon the purpose for which it was obtained and is retained in the firm.

In our earlier example, the sewing machines brought into the partnership by White would be Fixed assets.

If however the firm's business was trading sewing machines, then the machines would be included in stock and hence classified as Current assets.

THE PARTNERS' ACCOUNTS

A partner's Current account will be debited with the following entries:

* A share of any loss, determined in a Partnership Agreement
* Drawings
* Interest payable on any excess drawings
* Any Personal or private Expenses paid by the firm on his/her behalf

NB Salaries paid to partners are not debited to their current accounts since they are expenses of the business

A partner's Current account will be credited with the following entries:

* A share of profit as per a Partnership Agreement
* Interest on capital contributed
* Unpaid salary
* Interest on any Loan made by the partner to the firm

NB Note that any unpaid salary is credited to a partner's current account because it is a sum the business had agreed to pay, but for some reason did not.

LOAN ACCOUNTS

This third type of account is opened if a partner lends money to the firm, typically on a short term basis. The lender becomes a creditor of the firm of which he/she is a partner and is treated in the accounts in the same way as any other creditor.

It is important to remember that a loan by a partner is not a capital contribution and is therefore not to be treated as such in the accounts.

The lending partner may later capitalise the loan, i.e. convert the money into a capital contribution, or alternatively demand its repayment at an agreed date.

The three types of Account – Capital, Current, Loan, are shown in the firm's Balance Sheet, which we remember is a Statement of the financial position of a business at a given date – the end of the financial year.

It is a "snap-shot", and is not a part of the double entry accounting system.

Your accountant will advise on the most appropriate form of layout for the Profit & Loss Accounts and Balance Sheet. The same basic formats should be used every year, to facilitate comparisons between the constituent parts on a year-to-year basis.

As explained in chapter 5, the Capital "Employed" in a business is that capital used to generate the profit or loss for an accounting period, as calculated and shown in the Profit & Loss Account.

Capital Employed is conventionally shown under that descriptive heading, below which are then set out the various categories utilised and the Total Capital then displayed.

Below that is displayed the categories of where and how the capital is employed, in the section headed "Employment of Capital", and again a total struck.

As we know, for the Balance Sheet to balance, the Capital Employed must be equal to the Employment of Capital.

THE PROFIT AND LOSS ACCOUNT

We remember from chapter 5 that an important constituent part of a Balance Sheet is the profit or loss for the year. It will form a part of the partners' Current accounts because they have agreed to share it. It will also form part of the Capital Employed by the firm and thus appear in the Balance Sheet.

When calculated from the P/L Account, this profit or loss figure is carried forward to the Balance Sheet.

Since we are looking at partnership accounts, we will also need to know and show each individual partner's share of the profit or loss, calculated according to the agreement reached.

Calculating these sums involves an extension to the Profit & Loss account, showing how the net profit/loss for the year is apportioned between the respective partners. This is shown separately and identified as an Appropriation Account.

The Account is then called the Profit and Loss and Appropriation Account, not surprisingly.

The mode of presentation for an Appropriation account does not have to accord with any accounting convention.

The layout of how the profit has been calculated in the following example has been abbreviated, since it is fully explained in chapter 5. A profit sharing ratio of 60% (Smith) and 40% (Jones) is assumed.

PROFIT & LOSS AND APPROPRIATION ACCOUNT OF SMITH & JONES FOR THE YEAR ENDED 31 AUGUST 199–

		£
	INCOME	
	Sales	200,000
Less:	EXPENDITURE	
	Admin. Expenses, depreciation etc.	130,000
	Net Profit	70,000

APPROPRIATED AS FOLLOWS:

	Salaries	Interest on Capital	Profit Share	Total
Smith	NIL	3,000	36,000	39,000
Jones	5,000	2,000	24,000	31,000
	5,000	5,000	60,000	70,000

The share of profit is calculated as follows:

	Salary	Interest on Capital	Total	Net Profit 70,000
Smith	NIL	3,000	3,000	
Jones	5,000	2,000	7,000	
	5,000	5,000	10,000	(10,000)
Total of Remaining Profit =				60,000
Of which Smith at 60% =				(36,000)
and Jones at 40% =				(24,000)
				60,000

THE BALANCE SHEET

Returning to the Balance Sheet we can see how the necessary information from the P/L account is incorporated.

Below is an example of a Balance Sheet layout which illustrates the areas we have examined and shows the linkages between the two final accounts:

BALANCE SHEET OF SMITH & JONES AS AT 31 AUGUST 199-

		£	£
CAPITAL EMPLOYED			
Capital accounts:			
	Smith	30,000	
	Jones	20,000	50,000
Current Account **:			
	Smith	3,400	
	Jones	1,600	
			5,000
			55,000
EMPLOYMENT OF CAPITAL			
	Fixed Assets		34,000
	Current Assets	26,000	
Less:	Current Liabilities	(5,000)	
	Net Current Assets		21,000
			55,000

** Movements on Partners' Current Accounts

	Smith	Jones
	£	£
Opening balance (b/fwd) as at 1.9.199–	2,300	1,500
Salaries	NIL	5,000
Interest on Capital (10%)	3,000	2,000
Share of profit (60%–40%)	36,000	24,000
	41,300	32,500
Less: Drawings	(37,900)	(30,900)
Closing Balances	3,400	1,600

Notes To Accounts:

i) Notice how the Current Accounts are set out as a finalised calculation, and as we would expect, separate from Capital. These accounts are derived from the detailed calculations headed "Movements on Partners' Current Accounts", which show the extent to which the accounts have changed over the course of the financial year. They are shown as a subsidiary calculation to the Balance Sheet.

ii) Opening Balances on the Current Account calculations are shown for the sake of completeness, assuming that there was a Balance Sheet for the business in the previous year. The closing balances from the balance sheet of the previous year then become the Opening Balances in the current year calculations.

iii) Interest on Capital is calculated again at an assumed rate of 10%.

iv) The sub-totals of these figures are then deducted from the Profit figure (as in our previous example), taken from the Profit & Loss Account. This leaves the share of remaining profit to be apportioned according to the agreed rate,
60% – 40%.

v) The second sub-totals then show the total income from all sources to the account of each partner.

vi) Finally, the total Drawings of each partner for the year are deducted from their total income, since drawings represent "income on account", drawn throughout the course of the year. These final balances, since they remain within the business, form part of the Capital Employed.

vii) As we know, the purpose of the Balance Sheet is to illustrate how much capital is employed in the business and what it is employed on, to demonstrate that the one side is equivalent in money terms to the other and that the Balance Sheet balances.

viii) Notice the way in which "Employment of Capital" is set out and by convention sub-divided in the layout.

a) Fixed Assets
b) Current Assets
c) Current Liabilities

Current assets minus Current Liabilities gives us our Net Current Assets, sometimes referred to as "Working Capital".

	Fixed Assets
plus	Net Current Assets
=	Employment of Capital

Net Current assets less any Long-term liabilities would produce the firm's Net Assets.

CHANGES TO THE PARTNERSHIP

i) Membership

Changes in the membership of a partnership which then continues in business after the change have implications for the accounts.

Suppose a partner dies or retires, and/or another person comes in to the firm as a partner. In such cases it will be necessary to apportion the net profit:

a) for the period before the change; and

b) for the period after the change.

Apportionments of salaries, interest on capital and shares of remaining profit will need to be calculated for each accounting period that straddle the accounting year.

ii) Dissolution

Alternatively a partnership may simply dissolve and reform under another name, or dissolve permanently. In either case the assets of the dissolved firm must be realised, i.e. collected in, valued and then distributed.

Section 39 of the Partnership Act 1890 provides that the partners are entitled to use partnership property to pay the firm's debts and liabilities. The partners must also repay any money they might owe the firm. After this is done, any remaining surplus assets should be used to distribute to the partners what is due to them.

Subject to any Partnership Agreement, section 44 of the Act provides that the firm's assets shall be applied in the following order of priority. Each category must be paid off completely before moving to the next:

1. All debts and liabilities of the firm to persons who are not partners i.e. external creditors.
2. All debts of the firm owed to partners, as internal creditors e.g. loans.
3. To each partner his/her capital contribution.
4. Any remaining asset surplus must then be distributed among the partners according to their profit-sharing ratio.

Glossary of Accounting Terms

a/c	Abbreviation for Account
Accrual	A sum added to an account to reflect an asset or liability missing from the books at the point of preparing the accounts.
Accrued Expense	An expense item relating to the current period for which no invoice has been received and for which payment is not yet due. It will appear as a Balance Sheet creditor.
Accumulated Depreciation	The total aggregate depreciation charged on assets over their lifetime since acquisition.

Analysed Cashbook	The cashbook used to record the sources of income and recipients of money paid out. Additional columns are used on the Expenses side to facilitate detailed analyses of different types of expense.
Appropriation Account	The subsidiary account to the Profit & Loss Account setting out the distribution of Profit/Loss, to whom and how much. Used where there is more than one proprietor of a business.
Bad Debt	A sum owed to a business which is irrecoverable and must be written-off.
Balance Sheet	A "snapshot" financial picture of the assets and liabilities of a business at a specific point in time-usually the end of the financial year.
Bank Reconciliation	The exercise conducted to prove the balance shown in the books of a business is the same as the balance on the bank statement at the end of a period, usually each month.
Bought Ledger	Known also as a Purchase ledger.It shows

	the individual accounts with each supplier, recording money owing to them and how accounts have been settled with them.
Capital	The value that a business owes back to its owners. Remember that a business is separate from its owners, so capital is a liability of the business to them.
Capital Account	The account which records and monitors movements of capital within a business.
Capital Employed	The aggregate value of fixed and net current assets used to generate the profit of a business.
Closing Stock	The value of raw materials and/or finished goods held at the end of an accounting period. This will include the value of stationery, stamps etc purchased but unused in the current period.
Closing Work-in -Progress	Work in progress which has been been accumulated on behalf of customers at the end of the financial year but which has not been supplied nor invoiced.

Credit Sale	A sale for which payment is not made immediately at the time of supply, either to or by a business and for which an invoice will be raised later.
Creditors	Suppliers of goods/services who have not yet been paid for supplies made on credit.
Current Account	The account which shows the short-term money owed to the proprietor (as distinct from long-term Capital). Profit for the year is credited to the account and drawings on that profit debited. Generally only used in Partnership accounts.
Current Asset	An asset which will not be retained in the business in its present state for a long period of time. Includes stock, WIP, debtors, money at bank and petty cash.
Current Liability	A liability that is due to be paid within the following 12 months.
Debtors	Customers who owe money to the business.
Depreciation	The proportion of the value of a fixed asset that has been "used" in the current

	period to help produce a profit/loss.
Double Entry	The book-keeping system that ensures the accounts balance by requiring a corresponding equal debit entry for every credit entry on different accounts and vice-versa.
Doubtful Debt	A debt presumed to be irrecoverable at the time the accounts are compiled.
Drawings	In a sole proprietorship/partnership the amount of money withdrawn from the business for personal use.
Final Accounts	The Profit & Loss account and the Balance Sheet, drawn up at the end of the financial year.
Fixed Asset	A tangible asset of some permanence which will be used by the business over a long period of time, e.g. buildings/ machinery.
Goodwill	An intangible asset which makes the business worth more than the aggregate net value of its assets as shown in the balance sheet. Factors in calculating Goodwill include reputation and location.

Loan Capital	Long term liabilities of a business, provided by either the proprietor/s or external sources, e.g. banks.
Long Term Liability	The liability falling due for payment more than 12 months after the date of the Balance Sheet.
Net Assets	The equation that shows the proprietor's financial interest in the business. Calculated as Fixed assets plus Current assets less Current liabilities less Long-term liabilities.
Net Book Value	The cost of an asset less the accumulated depreciation charged on it.
Net Current Assets	The value of current assets less current liabilities.
Net Profit	Total Income of a business less all Expenses incurred. The sum reflects the proprietors' return on their time and investment in the business.
Nominal Ledger	Also known as the general ledger. The set of accounts kept by the business from

	which the Final Accounts are drawn up.
Opening Stock	Stocks in hand at the start of the current period.
Opening WIP	The value of work-in-progress at the start of the current period.
Overheads	Expenses which cannot be directly related to a particular sale and which must therefore be apportioned over all sales, eg insurance.
Partnership	The legal relationship between two or morepersons in a joint business venture.
P/L Account	Abbreviation of Profit & Loss account.
Prepayment	An expense paid in advance of when it falls due. Technically a debtor of the business.
Profit & Loss Account	The financial statement of account for a period which reflects how a business has earned its Income less the Expenditure incurred in generating that Income.

Profit Sharing Ratio	The proportion of unallocated profit agreed by partners to be shared between them.
Proprietor	The owner of a business.
Revenue	The Income of a business.
Sole Trader	A person who trades as an unincorporated business without partners.
Trial Balance	The aggregation of Credit and Debit balances drawn from the nominal ledger at the end of a period.The trial balance, when proved correct, is used to produce the Final Accounts.
Unpresented Cheques	Cheques drawn by the business but which have not yet been cleared through the banking system and therefore do not appear on the bank statement at the date of the reconciliation.
Work in progress (WIP)	The value of any work carried out but for which no invoices have been raised.

Working Capital	Alternative term for Net Current Assets.

USEFUL INFORMATION

The following are Publishers of a wide range of Business Accounts Stationery:

1 Tollit & Harvey. Publish the "Guildhall" series of Cashbooks and looseleaf ruled analysis sheets, in pack form.

2 George Vyner. Publish the "Simplex" series, including a VAT Record book, with worked example pages.

3 Safeguard Systems (GB) Ltd. Publish starter packs for small businesses.

4 Kalamazoo Business systems.

USEFUL ADDRESSES

1 The Institute of Company & Commercial Accountants
40 Tyndalls Park Road
Bristol B58 1PL
Tel 0117 9738261

2 The Institute of Chartered Accountants In England & Wales
Chartered Accountants Hall
Moorgate Place
Moorgate
London EC2 2BJ
Tel 0171 920 8100

3 The Institute of Chartered Secretaries & Administrators
16 Park Crescent
London W1N 4AH
Tel 0171 580 4741

4 Business Names Registrations PLC
Somerset House
Temple Street
Birmingham B2 5DN